6 = 9/2/03

THE FALL OF MILOSEVIC
The October 5th Revolution

DRAGAN BUJOSEVIC
AND IVAN RADOVANOVIC

palgrave
macmillan

First published in 2003 by PALGRAVE MACMILLAN™
175 Fifth Avenue, New York, N.Y. 10010 and
Houndmills, Basingstoke, Hampshire, England RG21 6XS.
Companies and representatives throughout the world.

PALGRAVE MACMILLAN is the global academic imprint of the Palgrave
Macmillan division of St. Martin's Press, LLC and of Palgrave Macmillan Ltd.
Macmillan® is a registered trademark in the United States, United Kingdom
and other countries. Palgrave is a registered trademark in the European Union
and other countries.
1-4039-6064-X hardback

Library of Congress Cataloging-in-Publication Data

Bujosevic, Dragan.
   [5. oktobar. English]
The fall of Milosevic : the October 5th revolution / Dragan Bujosevic
and Ivan Radovanovic.
      p.   cm.
Includes bibliographical references and index.
   ISBN 1-4039-6064-X (cl.)
   1. Yugoslavia—Politics and government—1992–   2. Coups d'etat—
Yugoslavia—Serbia.   3. Milosevic, Slobodan, 1941–   I. Radovanovic, Ivan.
II.   Title.

DR1318.B8513   2003
949.7103—dc21
                                                          2003041023

A catalogue record for this book is available from the British Library.

Design by Letra Libre, Inc.

First Palgrave Macmillan edition: April 2003
10 9 8 7 6 5 4 3 2 1

Printed in the United States of America.

CONTENTS

FOREWORD

This book describes the two hours on the afternoon of October 5, 2000, when the seemingly invulnerable hold on power that Slobodan Milosevic and his regime had built over 13 years was demolished. The book is the outcome of conversations with 60 people—politicians, police, soldiers, and members of the public—who were in Belgrade that day. Both before and after the crucial and amazing hours on October 5, these people, and many others, played various roles, some even by doing nothing at all, and made it one of the most memorable dates in Serbia's long and turbulent history.

The authors are aware that writing about historical events requires distance and an abundance of material, data, and documents. It is a job for historians. Thus, despite their ambitions, they focused on a single task: to reconstruct the events of October 5, by drawing on the accounts of the participants, laying them out and revealing them as far as possible, dispelling the abundant rumors, and, probably most important of all, demonstrating that October 5 was a personal story for every one of the hundreds of thousands of participants in an event now being described by a variety of names, from revolt and revolution to *putsch* and coup d'état.

There was certainly some kind of organization behind the demonstrations; the leaders of DOS, the Democratic Opposition of Serbia, tried, as best they could, to anticipate what would happen that day. There can be no doubt that the police and army defied the orders given by Slobodan Milosevic himself, and that a kind of "non-aggression" agreement existed between DOS and sections of the police even before October 5. It is equally certain that Bogoljub "Maki" Arsenijevic, the well-known Serbian rebel who had been arrested and beaten after initiating protests against Milosevic in 1999 and who captivated the public with his spectacular escape from a prison hospital, quite on his own decided to organize a group to set fire to the Parliament and Radio Television Serbia (RTS) buildings; that the now-famous bulldozer operator Ljubisav "Joe" Djokic made his decision to set off for RTS on the night of October 4 after consulting only a cup of coffee and a pack of cigarettes.

"I was so angry," Joe said, much later, talking to the authors of this book. His statement is one of many testimonies of frustration and fury, offered in as many interviews, that substantiate the claim that October 5 simply had to happen, whether on that day or another, whether stage-managed or spontaneously.

Those whose accounts have helped to unravel the events of October 5 include Yugoslav President Vojislav Kostunica; Serbian President Milan Milutinovic; the chief of staff of the Yugoslav Army, Nebojsa Pavkovic; Federal Foreign Affairs Minister Goran Svilanovic; Serbian State Security chief Radomir Markovic; Deputy Serbian Prime Minister Nebojsa Covic; Democratic Party President Zoran Djindjic; the leaders of New Serbia, Velimir Ilic and Milan St. Protic; the president of the Christian Democratic Party, Vladan Batic; the president of New Democracy, Dusan Mihajlovic; and the former Serbian tourism minister and president of the Belgrade Committee of the Yugoslav Left, Slobodan Cerovic.

Accounts of October 5 were also given by senior officers of the Serbian Ministry of Internal Affairs and members of special police units. Some of these wished to remain anonymous. This does not, however, affect the validity of their statements. Others, like the commander of the Police Brigade, Colonel Bosko Buha, and the inspector of the Internal Affairs Division of the city of Cacak, Zoran Boskovic, have allowed their full names and titles to be used. Some of the others, "common people," who shared with us their own part of the truth about October 5 were Milder, Gigo, and Sekula from Kraljevo; Igor and Dragan from Cacak; Marko and Ivan, members of Delije, the Red Star soccer team fan club; Peca from the old Belgrade area of Dorcol; Drs. Slobodan Ivanovic and Dragan Joksovic; citizens of Belgrade who beat police officers and citizens who protected them; members of Otpor, the student movement whose name means "resistance"; former police officers; employees of the old and new Radio Television Serbia; and firefighters called in to fight the blaze in the Yugoslav Parliament and Radio Television Serbia buildings.

This book is as authentic as are the accounts of these people. The authors have not altered them in any way. In some cases when people gave vastly different versions of the same event, their accounts were checked as far as possible, and the more credible version used for the book.

The authors are aware, however, that this is not the whole truth of October 5 and that many of those who gave their accounts were speaking with the restraint imposed by the positions they held and their lack of distance from the event.

All of them agreed to one basic condition: that their accounts would not be published in the form of interviews, but pieced together in a large mosaic, the story of October 5.

The authors extend their sincere gratitude to everyone they spoke to and especially the many anonymous people who helped them collect the most diverse pieces of information. Without them this book would have been so much the poorer.

—Belgrade
Dragan Bujosevic
Ivan Radovanovic

PROLOGUE

If Slobodan Milosevic had kept his promise, he wouldn't be under arrest, on trial at the Hague for war crimes and crimes against humanity, pining for his grandson, Marko, playing in a *dacha* on the edge of Moscow.

"I have no intention of doing that," said the president of Yugoslavia on December 12, 1998, when *Washington Post* correspondent Lally Weymouth asked him, "Are you going to change the Constitution so that you can serve another term? You're still a young man." This was one of the 233 questions she asked Milosevic, who had just sidestepped NATO's first threat to bomb Yugoslavia. He already had two Draconian laws under his belt. One eliminated the autonomy of Serbian universities and put them under the control of the Serbian government, which surely would have led to Milosevic's cronies stifling one of the few forums of openness; the second moved decisions concerning the courts to the bureaucracy—the administrative judgements increasing the speed and politicization of decisions, decreasing the likelihood of criticism of the government, particularly from the press.

He broke his word on July 6, 2000, hastily amending the Constitution of Yugoslavia to allow him to serve another six years as president. A year earlier the political parties that formed the basis of his regime—the Serbian and Montenegrin Socialists, the Yugoslav Left, and the Radicals—had given him carte blanche to change the Constitution. There were three key changes: the president of Yugoslavia would be elected by the people, rather than being appointed with the consent of the two federal units (Serbia and Montenegro); the president could be dismissed only by a two-thirds majority vote of members of the Federal Assembly, not half as before; and the Assembly was given the authority to dismiss ministers in the federal government, which previously could be done only by dismissing the prime minister at the same time. The effect of these changes was to increase the power of the president at the expense of the Parliament. The nature of the constitutional amendments made it clear that Milosevic's next step would be to stand again for election as president of Yugoslavia. He didn't want to risk having to solicit Parliament's opinions again. Even Federal Prime Minister Momir Bulatovic was surprised and asked whether it was proper for the government to launch an initiative to amend the Constitution an hour after the Assembly session had been scheduled. Milosevic simply had to succeed this time: he couldn't afford to repeat the failure of 1997 when the Montenegrin Socialists, with an unprecedented degree of seriousness, disengaged from his embrace.

Twenty days later, on July 27, Milosevic made his expected move: he called elections, both those he had to—for the Yugoslav Parliament and local governments—and the one he didn't yet need to schedule—for the president of Yugoslavia. His term of office was due to end on July 23, 2001. He could easily have let his parties go to the polls with no danger of losing anything, even if they were outvoted. As long as he was president of Yugoslavia, it was irrelevant whether his parties were the majority in the Parliament or whether he had the support of the prime minister. The local governments in particular were of no significance as they had been completely stripped of power. The reality was that Milosevic's power was independent, based on his control of economic rewards, the army, and the police.

Milosevic believed that his charisma had not yet worn thin. He had no serious opponent. Vuk Draskovic, the media darling and charismatic leader of the opposition who had been prominent in the 1996 demonstrations, wasn't going to return from exile in Budva, the tourist resort on the Montenegrin coast, where he had moved after two attempted assassinations. Zoran Djindjic, an early leader of the opposition Democratic Party, didn't stand a chance, having been depicted by the powerful regime-sponsored media as the darkest brother of the darkest devil; and Vojislav Seselj, the leader of the Serbian Radical Party and a close ally of Milosevic, simply wouldn't dare to engage in a duel with him. Not in Milosevic's wildest dreams did he see Vojislav Kostunica. Nor did his eyes and ears, the State Security Service. If scheduling the presidential election was Milosevic's first major mistake, the second was to underestimate Kostunica, who would prove too hard a nut to crack.

With arrogant self-confidence, Milosevic told the chief of staff of the Yugoslav Army, General Nebojsa Pavkovic, just a few days before the elections, that he would get 70 percent of the vote; in a perverse fit of generosity combined with disdain both for the man and for the ideal of free elections, Milosevic boasted he could even treat Vojislav Kostunica to a hundred thousand phantom votes from Kosovo. Milosevic failed to understand that his reputation, or more specifically how he was perceived by the people whose support he needed but took for granted, was being frayed by the effects of his being in power for 13 years: the devastation of the wars; the thousands of Serbs killed and wounded; the poverty; and the hundreds of thousands of Serb refugees all contrasted with the wealth of his family and cronies. His amending the Constitution, then calling for early presidential elections, and now treating these elections cavalierly only added fuel. The people's discontent was summed up in the popular saying: "I can't even say his name—fuck him." Those who felt this popular but as yet amorphous discontent were only waiting for a chance to show what they thought about the reign of Milosevic and his wife, Mira Markovic, so closely were the two identified, and so widely were they hated.

Milosevic had been preparing his victory since early spring. He had stepped up police harassment of the members of Otpor (Resistance), an organization led by youths whose poorly attended events were lent importance by the regime's repressive reaction, with frequent beatings and arrests even of adolescent members. He didn't understand that wielding police batons against Otpor's enthusiasm and persistence worked against him. Throughout Serbia the rural people were saying "If he's beating children, he must be powerless."

But Milosevic believed in his power and thought he was showing the voters the impotence of the opposition, especially by not allowing them to even steal a glimpse of his native town: he had the police cordon off Pozarevac on May 9 when the opposition wanted to hold a rally there. He barred the opposition's access to electronic media in Belgrade with a brutal takeover of the municipal radio and television station, Studio B. The broadcaster's repeater station on Mount Kosmaj had been destroyed by "unidentified criminals" in January, and in March the transmitter on Torlak, one of the hills surrounding Belgrade, met the same fate. He limited the circulation of non-regime newspapers by artificially creating a shortage of newsprint. With extensive control of the media Milosevic sought to shape public opinion in his favor, going so far as to tell the Serbs, who didn't have a glimmer of understanding about the NATO bombing, and resented it, that the opposition were servants of the West and were being paid by the only military alliance in the world to help it bring its soldiers to rule Serbia and Yugoslavia.

"They're traitors," roared Milosevic and his wife, Mira Markovic, warning that the punishment for traitors was death.

Confident that he had done everything necessary, Milosevic was certain of the victory he needed to crack open at least the smallest door leading to the normalization of relations with the West, which had stated that democratic elections were a precondition for improved political and economic interaction. For this reason alone he was keen to confirm his charisma, even before the expiration of his term of office, and even if all he was willing to permit was the form, not the substance, of free elections.

For their part, the 18 parties that made up the Democratic Opposition of Serbia (DOS) had no doubt that their presidential candidate, Vojislav Kostunica, would win and that they would win the federal and local government elections. They remained confident even after the president of Montenegro, Milo Djukanovic, stabbed them in the back by boycotting the elections and handing Milosevic 20 seats in the Chamber of the Republics and 30 in the Chamber of Citizens. Non-government organizations were also optimistic and rallied to convince the voters that not voting was the worst possible choice. Otpor, with its clenched fist slogan, displayed its succinct election slogan, "He's Finished," on nearly every wall, every traffic sign, every sidewalk, and every street in Serbia. Delije, the group of rabid Red Star soccer fans, chanted "Slobodan, kill yourself and save Serbia" at soccer matches. On the eve of the election, all of them sang in unison at the top of their lungs "Kostunica, save Serbia from the madhouse."

While the ruling Left cried hysterically, "The government is chosen by the people, not NATO," the opposition cynically replied with a reference to Milosevic's wife: "The government is chosen by the people, not Mira." Public opinion polls revealed that the majority of voters were wearing shoes more than ten years old, symbolic given that the decade of Milosevic's leadership had resulted in economic decline. They believed absolutely in Kostunica's Messianic qualities, as absolutely as they believed there was no future with Milosevic, either for Milosevic himself, the voters, Serbia, or Yugoslavia.

The euphoric wave of popular rebellion against the Milosevic-Markovic reign was swelling, and even DOS was afraid of it. Some leaders of DOS were convinced that Milosevic was heading for defeat at the elections, that he would falsify the results, and that the opposition would then be lynched by the people unless it took a direct stand against the usurper of popular choice. For this reason DOS decided a few days before the September 24 election that no fraud would be permitted. "Him or us," said the leaders. The Serbian roulette wheel began to spin, and the stake—as in Russian roulette—was life itself. Three days before the elections, the weekly *NIN* wrote that the major issue was not who would win but whether the changeover of power would take place peacefully.

Three hours after polling closed on Sunday, September 24, Nikola Dinic, a district court magistrate in the southern city of Nis, submitted his resignation from the Federal Election Commission. He explained his resignation: "When we began recording packages of votes from penal and correctional institutions, the security guards prohibited us from seeing the ballot papers, saying they were acting on orders from the president of the commission." This was a clear sign that Milosevic was preparing to rig the results, as he had done with no major consequences in 1996.

This was Milosevic's third mistake. Falsifying the elections and denying the population an opportunity to express discontent was a step too far. Changing the Constitution and calling for snap elections while denying the opposition any public role had generated hostility among the people, but at least they could believe that the elections would provide an opportunity to express themselves and their discontent. After all, Milosevic could have recognized Kostunica's victory, formed a federal government with Montenegro's Socialist People's Party and become prime minister, thus maintaining his establishment. Kostunica would have been a titular head of state without authority or power, and the West would have to meet its promises to the opposition to lift the sanctions in return for free elections, as failure to do so would play into Milosevic's hands. Milosevic, however, was not satisfied with a bird in the hand. He wanted both the eagle and the lion from the Yugoslav coat of arms. Thus the spokesman for the Socialists and the Yugoslav Left first announced victory for Milosevic and a majority in the Parliament. When Milosevic realized he could not steal so many votes, he ordered his spokesmen to say that he was in the lead, but that the presidential election would go to a second round. Finally, aware of the extent of his loss, Milosevic admitted, again through his mouthpieces, that Kostunica had the majority. The strategy had changed: there was no winner in the first round. Milosevic wanted the runoff at any cost.

The Democratic Opposition of Serbia and, more important, the Radicals and the Serbian Renewal Movement, claimed that no runoff was necessary: Kostunica had won the election. Belgrade was in no doubt, and the next day 20,000 people converged on Terazije Square to celebrate the end of the era of Slobodan Milosevic and Mira Markovic.

Two hundred yards away, in the Federal Parliament building, the Federal Election Commission continued trying to revise the will of the people. The ballot papers went directly to the Bureau of Statistics instead of to the Commission, and not until Tuesday evening was the opposition able to either see the election materials or was the ballot report read by the commission's president to the public. The commission's president was Borivoje Vukicevic, an old friend of Milosevic who had been rewarded for his earlier achievements in remodeling election results by being allowed to continue working in the judiciary to 74 years of age, despite the law requiring judges to retire at the age of 67. The report now showed 145,000 votes cast in Kosovo, although Socialist spokesman Nikola Sainovic had said on several occasions that only about 45,000 people had voted in the province. This was an extra hundred thousand votes for Milosevic. At one polling station in Podujevo, all 1,573 registered voters had cast votes for Milosevic, as had all 6,000 voters registered at polling place number 29 in Prizren. The opposition's objections to the strangely inflated numbers from Kosovo and the bizarre unanimity in various towns were dismissed by the Federal Election Commission. The casting vote in that decision came from Zvonimir Tomanovic, who was not even a member of the commission for presidential elections, but served on the commission for elections to the Chamber of Citizens of the Federal Parliament.

While the Federal Election Commission was busy stealing votes, Milosevic had his intermediary, Belgrade Socialists chief Ivica Dacic, convey a message to DOS through New Democracy member Tahir Hasanovic. On the morning of Tuesday, September 26, Hasanovic told Zoran Djindjic, the Democratic Party leader, that Milosevic was offering a second round and that if DOS refused it he would announce that he had won outright in the first round. Djindjic consulted the DOS leaders and together they went to Vojislav Kostunica, who had indisputably won the election for Yugoslav president. They told him the choice was his: they would go along with whatever he decided. Kostunica had enough evidence that the people had elected him. He would refuse to stand in the second round.

Milosevic rubbed his hands in glee. He would be the only candidate in the second round of the presidential election on October 8, and he would win. Should the opposition call for demonstrations, there were a thousand ways to crush it once and for all. The Federal Election Commission went to work and during the night of Tuesday, October 3, released the results: Kostunica had 48.22 percent of the vote and Milosevic 40.25 percent.

The next day a smiling Milosevic made plans for the second round of the election with the Socialist Party Central Committee and branch representatives. He wasn't perturbed by dissatisfaction and criticism from the provincial membership, even though their past support had been essential for Milosevic to withstand previous challenges, including the demonstrations in the 1990s, opposition from Party Secretary General Gorica Gajevic, and the dissent within the party when it appeared the first time. He already knew what the Federal Election Commission would say: Kostunica, 48.96 percent of votes; Milosevic, 38.62 percent.

The result of the general election was a victory for DOS in the Federal Parliament, and the Left was totally routed in local government elections. This only further increased the opposition's confidence that the people were behind them and not in favor of Milosevic. The stage was set for the final showdown with Slobodan Milosevic. Zoran Djindjic called for a general strike, confident that Serbia would come to a standstill by Monday.

Serbia began hurtling toward rebellion. On Friday, September 29, primary and secondary schools shut down, businesses throughout the country closed their doors, cinemas were dark, and roads were blocked. Seven thousand miners at the Kolubara strip mine in Lazarevac, a small town about 40 miles southwest of Belgrade, stopped mining coal for the thermoelectric power stations. Kolubara was to be the heart of the people's rebellion for the next five days. The opposition breathed a sigh of relief: for the first time in ten years of protests they had the workers on their side. The Democratic Opposition of Serbia drew up a roster: one of its leaders had to be with the miners at all times. Kostunica himself visited Kolubara twice in the following five days.

Serbia held its breath. A nervous Milosevic, quite uncharacteristically, addressed the public twice in three days. At a graduation ceremony at the Yugoslav Army Military Academy in Belgrade on September 30 he alleged that the enemies at home were preparing to call in foreign troops. State television edited footage of the event so that the jubilant family and friends of the graduating officers appeared to be applauding Milosevic. Two days later, in an address to the nation, Milosevic told the people, "I consider it my duty to warn of the consequences of activities supported and financed by NATO governments. It should be evident to all that they are not attacking Serbia to get at Milosevic but attacking Milosevic to get at Serbia."

By now it was clear, even to the Left, that for the Kolubara coal miners there would be no second round. On October 3, the Serbian government, citing "attempted sabotage," passed a decree obliging the Serbian Power Utilities, of which the mine is a part, to maintain a prescribed level of production. Police riot squad units arrive in Kolubara to ensure that minimum production was achieved and began by throwing the miners out of the pits. The miners immediately called a strike, refusing to concede the theft of their votes.

The special forces, Milosevic's Praetorian Guard, came to Kolubara. The police chief did not use them against the miners, fearing the miners were too strong. Or perhaps he doubted that the special forces would act if told to attack the miners. A police officer ironically reworked an old joke about the slow-witted: "The police have finally figured it out, too." It didn't take a genius to realize Milosevic had little support and his time was running out. It was October 4.

Milosevic tried to release the built-up pressure of the red-hot cauldron of Serbia as the Constitutional Court of Yugoslavia annulled the first round of the presidential elections. There would be no second round; instead there would be new elections, but perhaps not until the expiration of Milosevic's term in July 2001. Branislav Ivkovic, then minister for science in the Serbian government and head of the Socialists in the Belgrade municipality of Vracar, was astounded by the court decision. The DOS leaders, on the other hand, were not. The nakedness of Milosevic's ambition to stay in power and his willingness to tarnish all of Yugoslavia's institutions to do so was always clear to those who sought to look, and now it was obvious to those who had diverted their eyes. The fuse for a popular uprising, based on indignation and legitimate anger, had been lit.

The people of Serbia, driving in five columns from five directions in cars, trucks, buses, and other vehicles, began converging on Belgrade. Slobodan Milosevic and Mira Markovic had only one last resort: to stop them through intimidation and violence. Why the people were no longer intimidated and why there was relatively little violence and repression is the story of the one-day revolution that overthrew Milosevic. That day was October 5.

ONE

THURSDAY, OCTOBER 5

STOP THEM WITH WASPS

The Serbian Ministry of Internal Affairs at 101 Kneza Milosa Street in central Belgrade is a squat, washed-out building, and is one of the few in its neighborhood not hit during the NATO bombing. At exactly midnight, the telephone rang. The police colonel who picked up the receiver heard a terse message: "Plan Three: Take Wasps and Hornets with you." He put the phone down. The other officers in the room stared at him. Wasps are rocket launchers. Hornets are like bazookas.

"Plan Three," he told the officers. "They want us to kill them."

Silence fell on the room. Its walls were freshly painted in pale green, the new desks were brown, as were the lockers which almost reached to the high, white ceiling. On a small table next to the colonel lay a Glock pistol with 18 rounds in the clip. At his feet, on the carpet, a Heckler & Koch with 30 rounds, telescopic sights, and a silencer. A real fighters' room. For years the men who sat in it had looked death in the eye in Croatia, Bosnia, and Kosovo. Now they were looking at the floor. Four of them, all senior officers of the special police units, had been assigned the task of meeting the convoys of demonstrators who would arrive in Belgrade. The men they led were seasoned war veterans. "Plan Three," the order that had just been given by Police Minister Vlajko Stojiljkovic through Police Chief Ljubo Aleksic, meant that the convoys of buses, cars, and trucks should be fired on using the heaviest weapons at the disposal of the special units: machine guns, Wasps, and submachine guns. The officers in the room were very familiar with what happens when a grenade from a Wasp hits a bus. Everyone dies, incinerated at 3,600 degrees Fahrenheit in the exploding gases.

A few blocks away, a 29-year-old senior officer of the Democratic Party, Cedomir ("Ceda") Jovanovic, sleepy, covered in the telltale red rash of fatigue, was repeating to himself: "Okay, if the police fire, we fire back."

Ceda's face was on "wanted" posters, as were the faces of Zoran Djindjic, the president of the party, and Nebojsa Covic, leader of the Democratic Alternative, and God alone knew how many other leaders of the Democratic Opposition of Serbia (DOS). Ceda had been given precise information about the plan to arrest and execute him. "We'd already spoken to people who had orders to kill us and didn't want to do it. Some had already received advance payment for the job."

For Ceda, there was nowhere else to go on October 5. If the demonstrations failed, some of the hit men who'd received down payments on his assassination might want to collect the balance as soon as October 6. "That or prison," thought Ceda. There were already nine charges against him, most of them for "undermining the state," and he was facing a five-month sentence for the same charge.

He picked up the telephone, deliberately calling from the Democratic Party premises, counting on the wiretap. Calling to Serbian towns, checking on whether they were joining in.

"Uzice, are you ready?" he shouted. "How many of you are coming?"

"Cacak! Ready?"

"Subotica?"

The plan called for the people who would overthrow Milosevic to arrive in Belgrade, the capital of both Serbia and Yugoslavia, from five directions. On the Ibar Highway would be people from the towns of Cacak, Kraljevo, Uzice, Valjevo, Ljig, Milanovac, and Takovo; the southern highway would bring people from Nis, Vranje, Leskovac, Pirot, Zajecar, Negotin, Bor, Majdanpek, and Kragujevac; on the northern highway would be the people of Subotica, Novi Sad, Vrbas, Backa Palanka, and Sombor; from the west would swarm residents of Sabac, Mitrovica, Loznica, Sid, Ljubovija, and Zvornik; and from the northeast, the people of Pancevo, Zrenjanin, Kikinda, Becej, Kovin, and Vrsac.

In a village near Ljubovija, which isn't even accessible by road, the local priest and teacher gathered the farmers together on the evening of October 4. Belgrade journalist Milovan Brkic heard from his mother that same evening: "Son," she told him, "the priest and the teacher told us that the man has really cheated us out of the election."

"Yes, mother, he has," replied Brkic.

"Well, then, our boys are off to Belgrade in the morning to get him."

That was the message from this simple rural woman.

After ten years of Milosevic it was clear to Brkic that the final showdown was at hand. "It's going to be very nasty," he murmured.

"We could fire," the police colonel was thinking. "We could kill maybe a hundred of them. We could kill another hundred somewhere else. Then nobody would come to Belgrade."

He looked at the other officers, their faces all twisted into questioning grimaces. The colonel knew what the question was. "What then?" he thought. "Most probably, popular rebellion." He could see the other officers shared his view. "NATO would bomb us," he told them. Speaking of the NATO forces and other troops in Macedonia, Kosovo, Albania, Bosnia, and Herzegovina, he warned that "the forces on our borders would flood in from all sides. The cities would burn, we'd be fighting in the forests." The colonel shrugged his shoulders. "I don't know, that's what would probably happen."

TWO

MAKI'S MOLOTOV COCKTAIL

The police colonel was right. At least in part. At that same moment, at the Jojkic Canal near Borca, on the outskirts of Belgrade, on the bank of the Danube, Bogoljub "Maki" Arsenijevic, a self-taught painter of frescoes, was drilling his men for rebellion. About 20 of them were aiming Coca-Cola bottles at old boats in the canal. The bottles were filled with a mixture of Pils beer and vodka, with a burning rag in the neck of each. Maki's Molotov cocktails. Without the classic wick. Just a piece of rag soaked in wax and dipped in gas.

The first one thudded against the boat and bounced off into the murky water.

"Fuck that," said Maki. "Throw another one. Harder!"

The second bottle hit the rudder and smashed. The canal flared up, lighting the flame of the self-taught people's rebellion. Maki and the guys, seven yards away from the bank, had to step back.

"Fucking great!" thought Maki. "That's how the Parliament will burn." Maki was in no doubt. "It's brutal," he said later. "You react like an animal. They do this, you do that."

That brutal urge had been building inside him for years. Then, on July 12, 1999, St. Peter's Day, he attacked the Valjevo town hall. The harsh treatment he received in prison after his attempted rebellion had not broken him. "They do this, you do that," he repeated. "Like an animal." He escaped from the prison hospital with a broken jaw, climbing down a rainspout out the window. Since then he had been in Borca, planning street conflict, setting fire to the symbols of Milosevic's power, and awaiting his own death.

None of the men drilling for revolution on the canal that night thought they would come out of it alive. Maki, their leader, had warned them, and they were prepared.

Milosevic would be waiting for them the next day, they were sure, with heavy weapons. In the reflection of the flames from the canal Maki was thinking, "We'll be killed, but the thing will happen"—Milosevic would be overthrown. The flames flared up. "They do this, you do that." The man who would set fire to the Federal Parliament 16 hours later was content.

Ceda Jovanovic dressed in his battle gear. Nike sneakers, wide black trousers with large pockets on the sides, the flak jacket that had been a necessity for days, a sweater, and a thin, rustling jacket. This outfit had been one of Ceda's trademarks since the days he had led the student demonstrations against Milosevic's stealing of local elections through the three winter months of 1996 and 1997. The Milosevic regime had used police violence to repress the demonstrations, but the students at Belgrade University, led by Ceda, had not backed down. Milosevic had been forced to admit that the elections were stolen, and thus Ceda Jovanovic had been the first opponent of Milosevic who had succeeded in besting him.

"When they see me like this everybody knows it's the battle plan. There'll be fighting and running."

The leaders of the five convoys had confirmed that everything was going according to plan. They were on the move. The way Ceda was dressed demonstrated his confidence that they would arrive, that the police resistance on the roads to Belgrade would be crushed.

"When the convoys arrive," he thought, "the police in Belgrade won't have anything to do." He thought the police must be having doubts. They would be asking themselves, "Well, what are we? The last defense? Whose?"

Ceda called for a car. Everything seemed to be going to plan.

About 300 yards away, in Beogradjanka, one of the city's tallest buildings, black by day and by night, a man stood looking at the lights of the Democratic Party headquarters, not at all sure that everything was going according to plan.

But Captain Dragan, a Western-educated military man, wasn't in charge of that. His task was another part of the activities planned for that day. A popular military hero, he had been the commander in just the same way in the early 1990s, in the newly founded rebel Republic of Srpska Krajina, after it had seceded from Croatia. During that operation, he and his men had reached the outskirts of the Croatian capital, Zagreb. Now he was sneaking his troops, dressed in civilian clothing, into Beogradjanka. "If everything goes as planned," he thought, "I'm going into action." But only if everything went as planned. Captain Dragan was known for not taking risks and he had no intention of taking risks here, when his job was to take over the building housing Studio B, the most important local television station in Serbia. Particularly when the building and the television station were guarded by about one hundred armed police.

His plan was brand new. Four hours old, to be precise. It had taken shape at exactly 8.00 P.M. on October 4, when his closest friend, Milan Stevanovic, a member of the Democratic Party, came unannounced to his apartment.

"Listen, Studio B is very important for us. We think there'll be about 50 or 100 armed police guarding it tomorrow. I've spoken to [Democratic Party president] Zoran Djindjic and suggested you lead the operation to remove the police from the building. What do you need for the job?"

Captain Dragan replied that he needed about 280 armed men. He wanted to have significantly greater strength than the police he was going to attack. Maybe the mere show of strength would avert bloodshed.

He began sneaking them in at 11 P.M. By morning, there were 130 of the captain's men inside Beogradjanka, nowhere near as many as he had wanted. He had hidden them in his offices—Captain Dragan has a large Internet center in the 24-story building. He gave them sleeping bags, banned smoking, and took the identification cards of all those who had been issued with weapons "to make it easier to collect them later." His guards posted on the lower floors interrupted him: "The police are coming in," they told him. He ordered them to turn off the lights.

Nine miles away, the suburb of Zeleznik was lit up. Ten thousand people were gathered in front of the hall where Nebojsa Covic's team played basketball. He was once a playmaker. Now he was a playmaker again, but this game was more important and there were a lot more players on the team. As many as 150 heavily armed men, most of them former police who had been fired over the past few years, had joined Covic, a former rising star of Milosevic's Socialists. The people in front of the hall were special security. They would stay there until the morning, and then head for Belgrade. Covic's name was also on the "wanted" list for organizing the miners' strike in Kolubara, but he wasn't the slightest bit nervous. It had been barely two days since his encounter with the special police units sent to arrest him.

There, on the outskirts of Zeleznik, he had spoken to policemen for two hours.

"No interference?" Covic finally extended his hand to a grim-faced policeman.

"No interference," the policeman accepted the hand.

"Not even on the fifth?"

"Not even on the fifth."

In hindsight, despite the importance of deals like this made by Covic and other DOS leaders with the police, it is clear that the move that won the game against Milosevic was something else.

Milosevic knew it too, which is why he was so determined to arrest his former acolyte and put him out of the game. Covic had organized the strike in Kolubara, and members of the Democratic Christian Party of Serbia had also been among the leaders of the strike. Two significant things happened in Kolubara: the first was that the police, faced with the demonstrators, showed their weakness and lost their bite; the second was that Belgrade, the sleeping capital of Serbia, finally awoke.

It had looked as if it would go on sleeping.

THREE

THE BATTLE OF KOLUBARA

"Somebody must come!" shouted the journalist on Radio Lazarevac. "Please, there are too many police. They're going to attack! They're going to attack!" Her voice shook Belgrade on Wednesday, October 4, at about noon.

"Oh, my God, they're going to kill them!" cried Jelena Carnaus of New Belgrade. "Let's go! Let's go!" she called to her sister, who was already putting her sneakers on.

Thousands of people reacted the same way that day. Convoys from Belgrade, decorated with stickers saying "Catch Geda" (a reference to a lazy, corrupt, thieving character who ruins everything), "He's finished," and "Blockade," set off to help the miners.

Bosko Buha, the commander of the Belgrade Police Brigade, didn't know at that moment whether anybody would reach Kolubara. His day had gotten off to a terrible start. "This is very nasty," thought Buha. First the news that he had to go to Kolubara. And then the scouts. The men he had sent to the mine, almost 40 miles away, to check the situation out had returned after two hours. Vladimir Ilic, his deputy, the leader of the reconnaissance unit, had walked through the door, torn his badge off, and thrown it on the table. "Here's my resignation," he said. "I can't do it."

"What can't you do?" asked Buha, his day now looking seriously bad.

"I can't fire at the miners," said Ilic. "I won't."

"What do you mean, fire at the miners?" Buha stood up. "Who's going to fire at the miners?"

"We are," said Ilic. "That's the order."

Buha sat down again, not quite sure whether this day should have begun at all. "Nobody's going to fire," he said slowly, waving at Ilic to sit down. "I'll go there myself." He pulled on his boots. "Nobody's going to fire."

The Police Brigade was about 700 strong. They had armored combat vehicles, 12.9 mm heavy machine guns, Wasps, Hornets, all kinds of automatic weapons, water cannons, and, most important, extraordinary war experience from operations in Kosovo. The brigade was stationed in special barracks in the Banovo Brdo neighborhood of Belgrade. This would become important the following day when the unit decided to transform itself into a "people's militia." Buha took 200 men to Kolubara with him. Ten percent of them had rifles, while others had revolvers, shields, and truncheons.

As he led the police motorcade in a heavy four-wheel-drive vehicle along the rutted Ibar Highway toward the Kolubara strip mine, two thoughts nagged Buha. One, if he disobeyed orders he would be dismissed and maybe worse. Two, he had no intention of carrying out such orders.

"What the hell," he decided. "I'll do it and I won't."

The police had already massed in front of Kolubara. From the distance Buha recognized the voice of General Obrad Stevanovic of the Ministry of Foreign Affairs. "There's Colonel Zivanovic," he said to Major Nebojsa Pantic, an officer with the Belgrade Police Brigade who was in the vehicle with him. He also saw Colonel Nikola Curcic, the commander of the Serbian government's new anti-terrorist units.

"This is really a nasty day," Buha told himself. "A seriously nasty one."

"The police are going into the mine! The police are going into the mine! They're armed!" cried the Radio Lazarevac reporter.

People from Cacak, Mladenovac, and Valjevo were rushing toward Kolubara.

Djordje Vlajic, a BBC radio journalist, was already at the mine, next to the administration offices, a neat building 100 feet long and more than half again as wide. It was connected by an awning to a similar construction, the mess hall, and surrounded by a park with pine trees spreading most of the way around. From the offices, the sloping conveyor belt could be seen, a steel contraption like a fun-fair slide. In normal times it carries tons and tons of coal on a slow journey.

When the portly Buha entered the mine, in heavy police fatigues, there were about 300 or 400 police in front of the offices. He knew that the 50 or so police with riot shields and long batons would only have to shout "Boo!" and there wouldn't be a soul left in the buildings.

Familiar with such encounters, Vlajic immediately looked Buha and the officers with him in the eye. Usually, Vlajic knew, police officer's faces reveal what they're planning to do. "They're not going to do anything," he concluded calmly, entirely unaware of the grave orders Buha had just received.

Buha took about 50 men right up to the building. General Stevanovic had ordered Buha to move the miners working the morning shift out of the mine at any cost. "By half past one," Stevanovic had said. The second shift of miners was due soon after that, and their arrival would make any operation to remove the miners much more difficult.

"Be careful, they have weapons. Be careful. They'll shoot," the officers told Buha and his men. Buha frowned. "That's the way to do it," he thought ironically; he had spent enough time at the front line to know what prompted people to begin killing. "They're scared, they've got a bullet in the barrel and when one goes off somewhere—once the first round is fired, there's chaos."

Buha had other ideas. When he got out of the general's earshot, he called Major Pantic to him. "We're going into the mine. Listen to me: no firing and no killing." Pantic nodded. "If anybody fires at us," said Buha, looking his officer straight in the eye, "we'll first run for cover and then we'll see whether it was some idiot shooting or something else. Understood?"

He didn't need to ask. It had been Pantic who, the day before, had defused the situation when police confronted students demonstrating in Belgrade. The orders had been similar to those he received today: Crush them. Instead, Pantic had guarded the students on their march through Belgrade.

Buha made it clear, nonetheless, mostly for his own sake: "Be careful. If you find anyone there, be pleasant, polite, kind. Explain to them that it's our job to take them out and if we can't . . . we'll think of something. You understand?"

Pantic understood. So did their men. That's what BBC reporter Vlajic saw on their faces as they slowly approached the mine's administration building. So he wasn't surprised when they asked the miners, kindly, to leave—just leave the building.

That was at about noon, and Buha was looking impatiently at his watch. "A bad day," he muttered, "and a long one." One-thirty seemed a long way off.

"Who are they?" Major Pantic wondered, as he saw people coming from the open cuts, down the brown hills, toward the police and the administration building—ragged and sooty people, about 150 of them.

"Jack-in-the boxes," laughed Vlajic.

"You're going to fire!" a French reporter suddenly screamed at Pantic.

"For God's sake, madam," replied the major. "You really think so, at our own people?"

The miners who had just arrived from the mile-wide strips of Kolubara asked to talk to Buha. Buha also asked to talk to them. He recognized some of them from the village of Miroseljac, in Sopot, where he had once been chief of police.

The miners called him by his nickname. "Bole, Bole!" He waved.

He was trying to look serious. "I'm still some kind of policeman," he thought. He was furious at the whole day, himself, and whomever had made this huge mess.

The cell phone brought him down to earth. "Get rid of them! Get rid of them!" it screeched. "Hurry up, before the second shift arrives!"

"Okay," Buha replied slowly, "I'll do it right away." He turned to the miners and said, loudly enough for others, including those on the phone, to hear him: "You have five minutes to get out." As soon as he mentioned minutes, he felt nauseous. The clock ticking in his stomach made every second seem a full minute.

"The police have set a deadline of five minutes!" cried the Radio Lazarevac reporter. "Then, they're going to intervene!"

The united Serbian cities dispatched extra convoys to Kolubara. Those already on the road stepped on the gas. But BBC journalist Vlajic saw nothing threatening at the mine all that time. No ugly words, no ugly looks.

"We don't want a fight," the miners said.

"Nor do I," replied Buha, looking at his watch. Only 15 minutes had passed. There was still half an hour to go before the 1:30 shift arrived. "A very slow day," he thought, looking at the miners. What will they say?

"We'll resist passively, like Gandhi," they told him.

"Then I'll have to carry you out," said Buha, looking above their heads. They pointed to a man who weighed at least 300 pounds.

"What the hell," said the colonel, "I'll take him out too."

He had to think of something. Some kind of show. Something that would be significant both for them and for him and that would at least speed up the passage of time. His stomach was churning. His mobile phone was ringing. The walkie-talkie was hissing at him. Then he saw what he'd been looking at the whole time. "How could I miss it?" he thought. "How?"

"I see there are holes in the fence," the colonel said to the Gandhi-like miners.

"There are."

"So why don't you . . ." Buha wanted them to get the idea straightaway. "Why don't five or six of you go out through the gate and then back through the hole? Do you understand?"

The miners looked perplexed.

"Out and in, you understand?" the colonel repeated. "So that I can do my job a little bit?"

After that, things went smoothly. The miners went out the gate in small groups, then circled round and came back through the fence to the mine. "They're leaving," Buha shouted into his cell phone. "I'm going to take the buildings now, too." The miners were standing peacefully around. "That's good, let him secure the buildings," they said to Vlajic.

A number of women came out of the administration building. Buha offered to transport them to the highway. He gave orders into the mobile phone. "Here, the crushing plant and the administration buildings, the transformer station, the mess hall. Let's do it easy. Why should I hurry? And if there were explosives planted in there? Look here."

And then, on the radio, he heard that there were serious problems at the police roadblocks around the mine.

In order to reach the Kolubara mine you have to leave the Ibar Highway near Stepojevac, then follow an even worse road for less than a mile to the small bridge over the Kolubara River. The mine is less than a mile beyond the bridge.

The police roadblock at the Kolubara bridge consisted of a cordon of policemen, the "Black Marias" (police vehicles for holding prisoners), and a number of police cars.

A camera crew from Belgrade's TV Mreza recorded the scene as the police roadblock fell apart.

First, somebody jumped into a bus parked near the bridge, started it, and crashed into one of the Black Marias. The police hurriedly positioned their buses on the bridge and got behind them. But their roadblock of buses was no match for the bulldozer that lumbered onto the bridge. To be precise, it was a multi-purpose crushing vehicle, with a large scoop and large wheels: The following day, a slightly different version would become the symbol of the whole revolution.

The bulldozer swept the buses aside with its scoop. Policemen, batons at the ready, ran at the bulldozer, dodging a hail of bottles and stones. The police halted, shouting, "Don't do this!"

But by then a mob of opposition supporters had arrived at the bridge from Belgrade, Cacak, Milanovac, Valjevo, Obrenovac, and Ljig. They rolled up their trousers, took off their shoes, and waded into the Kolubara River under the bridge. The police cordon moved back.

"There are people coming! There are people coming!" The Radio Lazarevac reporter was out of her mind with happiness.

BBC journalist Djordje Vlajic remembers the first groups of rescuers arriving at the administration building, their faces flushed, their trousers wet. Then cars and buses full of them swarmed in. The evening was rapidly drawing in and to Colonel Buha it seemed far more beautiful than the long day that had just passed.

Night had fallen by the time General Stevanovic arrived at the mine and commended Buha for a job well done. At that time there were more than five thousand people at the mine. Vojislav Kostunica was talking to the media and the miners in the administration building. The Kolubara story was over.

"The teeth of the police were pulled at Kolubara," current Deputy Serbian Prime Minister Nebojsa Covic said later. "They chased the miners around the pits, they tried everything, but they didn't manage to do anything. Not a single unit intervened at Kolubara, unless you call pushing and shoving an intervention. The blade was blunted there."

President Vojislav Kostunica was asked for this book whether he believed, that Wednesday evening in Kolubara, that he would win the following day, October 5, in Belgrade. "I was confident," said Kostunica, the new president of Yugoslavia.

A few other points should be made about Kolubara.

Some days later, when everything was over, Colonel Buha pieced together the chain of command that—had it held together—could have led to a massacre of the Kolubara miners. The idea of firing at them had come from Slobodan Milosevic himself. He conveyed his wishes to Police Minister Vlajko Stojiljkovic, who passed it on to Police Chief Ljubo Aleksic, who passed it on to General Stevanovic, who relayed the order to Colonel Zivanovic.

According to the plan, once Buha got rid of the miners, strikebreakers would be brought in to work the mines. These had been gathered wherever they could be found, even in the prisons. Early in November a convict from the Zabela prison in the city of Pozarevac told a television crew that he had been given seven days of solitary confinement "because I didn't want to go to some mine, Kolubara, to work there."

The state television cameras were also standing by near Kolubara. They were ready to go into the mine with the strikebreakers and film the sham miners and coal moving on the conveyor belts. Immediately after that, on the evening news, the most important political news program for the Milosevic regime, there was to have been an announcement of the end of the strike that the authorities would claim had left Serbia without electricity.

Even if the miners had been gotten rid of, however, the rest of the plan was likely doomed for reasons Milosevic could not anticipate. The miners had told Buha, while they were running around the mine with him and the police, that they had removed essential parts from all the machinery, the conveyors, the loaders, transformer stations, and the crushing plant. "God himself could not have got the coal moving," they said.

Kolubara had been well organized—or at least as well as it is possible to organize anything in this country, said Nebojsa Covic, current deputy Serbian prime minister. "Insofar as you can organize anything in Serbia, it's important to arrange the basics and to choose the right people, people who can't be scared off, who won't crumble under pressure or threats; you just let them go and then a miracle happens."

One of the miracles was most certainly the fact that Covic had monitored the whole visit of General Nebojsa Pavkovic, chief of staff of the Yugoslavian Army, to the Kolubara miners, three days before, using his mobile phone.

Another miracle surely was the surprising effectiveness of the most potent weapon used in Kolubara: radio. The screams of the Radio Lazarevac reporter were heard in Belgrade thanks to Radio 988, a music and sports station established two years earlier by Covic. It had begun broadcasting a current affairs program on October 2, only two days before the Kolubara standoff. The broadcasts on October 4 directly influenced the Belgrade suburbs of Cukarica, New Belgrade, Zemun, as well as the areas stretching along the Ibar Highway toward Lazarevac—in other words, toward Kolubara and the mines.

Student broadcast Radio Indeks and Radio B2–92 took over from Radio 988 and alerted the rest of Belgrade. Someone tried to jam the broadcasts with a signal from a karate club in Zemun that was run by Dragoljub Kocovic, a member of the Yugoslav Left's Central Committee. Covic's mobile teams thwarted the disruption. A higher intensity signal from Sremcica was targeted at the Belgrade suburb of Zemun.

That was enough. Belgrade woke up. And that's how the battle for Kolubara was won.

FOUR

VLAJKO STOJILJKOVIC, THE "MILITARY COMMANDER"

On Thursday, October 5, sometime after midnight, under the fluorescent lights of the pale green room, the colonel and his officers didn't need much discussion to come to an agreement. There was no way they would carry out their orders. Nor could they disobey them.

"If we disobey," the colonel said, "we'll be thrown out of the service." The officers were silent. He made it very clear: "If we don't do it we'll be disciplined for disobeying orders." The officers nodded in agreement.

They were prepared for the charge. In any case, they were fed up with everything. Especially politics. And Milosevic. The battles they'd won for him and the wars they'd lost for him. And with Police Minister Vlajko Stojiljkovic. "He thinks he's a military commander," said one of the officers sarcastically.

In their favor, on October 5, was the fact that the game was already over in the Serbian Ministry of Internal Affairs. The chain of command had been broken. The word around the ministry building was that General Vlastimir Djordjevic, the head of public security, had already said about Milosevic, a few days previously: "He's lost the elections and should step down. It's easier for him to step aside than for the whole nation."

After that, Djordjevic was dropped from the chain of command. Stojiljkovic, as police minister, was calling police units and issuing orders. The problem was that his authority with the police was non-existent. The only thing on the officer's minds was how to avoid their orders.

The colonel called his people in Uzice and Sabac. He told them about the Wasps and the Hornets. He knew that this was the toughest assignment they'd ever been given. "You're not stupid," he said, "you know what that means." He had no doubt that they would understand what he'd told them. Plan Three would have been a disaster. He also gave his officers their orders. He told his people in Uzice and Sabac that they would hear from him through another contact. Milosevic's time was running out.

Goran Svilanovic, the leader of the Civil Alliance of Serbia and soon-to-be Yugoslavia's minister for foreign affairs, was ravenous with hunger that evening. The last few days had flown past like an assembly line: tours, meetings, plans, no food, no sleep. The Democratic Opposition of Serbia (DOS) had put him in charge of Uzice. He thought about food somewhere along the long, rutted, and completely jammed Ibar Highway.

"Look at that," Svilanovic exclaimed to his fellow passengers when they reached the town of Preljina. "It's magnificent!"

They barely managed to weave through the hundreds of large trucks. The truck drivers waved their hands in the Serbian three-fingered salute. The same drivers, a few days earlier, when the police had come to move them, had hoisted a police car into the air with their bare hands. The army's troops weren't only blocked at Preljina, near Cacak. Svilanovic was confident: "The whole of Serbia is rising."

Svilanovic was badly in need of food. There are scores of hash houses along the Ibar Highway between Belgrade and Uzice. "Roast Lamb!" "Barbecue!" "Roast Meat!" screamed the flashing signs, the enormous grills in some places almost butting onto the highway. "And not one of them open!" The grill houses of Serbia were on strike, all the way to the Durmitor.

"Stop!" he shouted. "Food!"

The grill house at the Durmitor was empty. There hadn't been a single customer all day in the only restaurant open on the whole Ibar Highway.

"What's up?" Svilanovic was puzzled by the empty tables.

"Well, look what they're doing," complained the man inside, the restaurant's owner by the look of him. Then Svilanovic saw the photograph of Slobodan Milosevic on the wall above the man's head. He turned and went back to the car. "Let's get moving," he said curtly. His stomach growled.

He ate his fill in rebellious Uzice. In the Civil Alliance headquarters, women were preparing packed lunches. Hundreds of them. Fresh bread, the local smoked ham, and *ajvar,* a salad of chopped eggplant and peppers. "Wonderful, wonderful!" Svilanovic said over and over again as he ate. People were coming to the Civil Alliance. They were bringing their winter pickles, juices, money, whatever they had. Some brought twenty dinars. One private entrepreneur contributed one thousand Deutschmarks.

Svilanovic was content. He fell asleep with a full stomach and a full heart. Uzice, awake and busy throughout the night, had given him a clear message: "We're going to win!"

Far away from Uzice, in the outer Belgrade suburb of Obrenovac, Vladan Batic, the leader of the Democratic Christian Party, lit a candle from the Ostrog Monastery and prayed that Milosevic would fall without bloodshed.

In Belgrade's neighborhood of Banovo Brdo, Ljubisav Djokic, known as Joe, was sitting in the dark, smoking, angry at the police and the authorities. He decided that he'd take his bulldozer in the morning. "Even if it gets me killed," Joe said to himself as he stubbed out his cigarette. He had no inkling that the next day he would become a symbol of revolution.

In the center of the city, Democratic Party President Zoran Djindjic left the party building.

A new hour of the great day had begun. General Nebojsa Pavkovic, the chief of staff of the Yugoslav Army, was sleeping peacefully.

FIVE

DJINDJIC MEETS LEGIJA

"Let's go," said Zoran Djindjic, and about ten young men with rifles ran out into sleepy Proleterskih Brigada Street in Belgrade. The man behind much of the Democratic Opposition of Serbia (DOS) strategy was heading for a meeting with a senior police official. He left the building without a flak jacket, but feeling much better than he had seven hours earlier when he had left the party premises by himself.

That had been the condition for a meeting with the commander of the Serbian State Security's Special Operations Unit. "Admirala Geprata Street," Milorad "Legija" Ulemek, the chief of the Red Berets, had said. "And come alone. No escort."

"He could kill me," Djindjic thought of Legija, as he walked through the streets of Belgrade in the twilight. But it didn't even cross his mind not to go. He was pragmatic: "It's worth the risk. If there's anything I can do it's here and now. Later the price will be higher."

In any case Djindjic trusted him. Before the first round of the elections, Special Operations Commander Legija had told him that his men were not involved in any irregularities. They were in their barracks, going about their regular duties. And he hadn't lied. "Anyway," thought Djindjic, "It was he who invited me this time. I ought to go." He'd already reached Admirala Geprata Street. Legija's people were standing in the shadows of the tall buildings. Djindjic got into an armored jeep. They drove around the city.

"It's going to be a mess," said Legija. "The orders are extreme."

Djindjic was calm. "All right. What should we do?"

"Don't fire at the police. Don't charge the barracks." Legija was curt.

"All right," promised Djindjic, "We won't."

"Your word?"

"My word."

Much later, giving his account for this book, Zoran Djindjic admitted that the Red Berets had been his greatest fear. "When he told me that, as far as they were concerned, there wouldn't be any intervention, it was a load off my mind."

By the time he got out of the jeep he was finally convinced that he would win. He could go more calmly to his 1 A.M. meeting at the Ministry of Internal Affairs. And finish it more quickly. He only needed to hear two things:

"We have been ordered to use the Wasps and the Hornets," the senior police officer told him.

"And?" asked Djindjic.

"And we're not going to obey it."

On his way back from the meeting, the manager of the revolution, as he was later dubbed by Western journalists, had the whole plan unfolding in his head. Piece by piece. It seemed to him that it was coming together.

The outline of the plan had been prepared four or five days before the first round of the election. In a dark room in Nebojsa Covic's metalwork factory, reeking of cooking smells but protected against wiretaps, the DOS leaders resolved for the first time: "This is make-or-break."

They knew that Milosevic wouldn't acknowledge an opposition victory and that they would have only five or six days to get rid of him without protest marches or daily demonstrations. That was why they decided on a strike this time. And roadblocks.

A little socialism and a little student action, that was the whole of the strategy. Believing that Milosevic would rig the vote in Belgrade but that DOS would have an absolute victory in Novi Sad, Cacak, and Nis, they agreed that the opposition should barricade themselves in those cities, demonstrate for seven or eight days, throw roadblocks up around the capital, and end the whole thing with a march on Belgrade.

"The winner will stay, the loser will be finished, both physically and as a party," said Djindjic, explaining this part of the plan.

The "students and socialism" strategy had more serious elements. There was an idea for a strike in Kolubara and the Motors and Tractors Industry in New Belgrade. The miners were to protest in the mine while the New Belgrade workers demonstrated in front of the Yugoslav Parliament. Only the first part of this idea materialized.

Having made their plan, all that was left for DOS was to wait. Djindjic predicted four "election attacks" by the Milosevic regime. The first, against the DOS polling observers, didn't happen. The second, disconnecting telephones on election night, didn't happen either. Nor did the third, stuffing the boxes with fake ballot papers and proclaiming the elections null and void. Djindjic's fourth prediction was that the Left's observers would refuse to sign the count. They signed.

"He's finished," thought Djindjic on the night of September 24. He began to prepare for an uprising. It was the only option left. Nobody believed that Milosevic would concede defeat.

"Everyone off to their towns," Djindjic told the Democratic Party leaders, "and get ready." He thought that Milosevic would begin arrests and proclaim a state of emergency. "He might even have some of us killed," he told his people.

A showdown with the regime was now unavoidable, and detailed planning was required. On the evening of September 26, the DOS leaders unanimously decided to respond with whatever level of force was used against them by the police. The decision was made "despite the possible consequences." Vojislav Kostunica was not present at the vote, the only DOS leader not there. But he had expressed his reservations about this plan before he left the meeting.

Nebojsa Covic, Zoran Djindjic, and General Momcilo Perisic, the former chief of staff of the Yugoslav Army who now headed the Movement for a Democratic Serbia, had been chosen to run the operation. Until it was all over, only these three would know exactly what was supposed to happen on October 5.

SIX

ATTACK PLAN, DEFENSE PLAN

The plan was divided into several phases. One of the first was devoted to self-defense and arming the people. Democratic Party leader Nebojsa Covic was rightly accused by the regime of procuring a trailer-load of weapons. He, Democratic Party President Zoran Djindjic, Vladan Batic, leader of the Democratic Christian Party, and Velimir "Velja" Ilic, the co-president of New Serbia, organized task forces. These were made up of former police-men and soldiers, well armed and sufficiently cool headed. Not everyone knows how to talk to the police, how to overpower an armed man, when to throw tear gas, and when to pull a gun.

The roadblocks were another story. The greatest danger was that the police could throw all their force at the roadblocks and smash them at the outset. For this reason it was decided that they should be as far as possible from Belgrade, where DOS would be strong enough to defend them. The most impressive blockade was that on the Ibar Highway, near Preljina. It was set up by about one hundred truck drivers from Cacak. The police didn't dare approach it.

The decision for five convoys to converge on the capital from five regions of Serbia was made on October 3. Leaders were allocated to each convoy: Momcilo Perisic, leader of the Movement for a Democratic Serbia, would head the Nis convoy; Goran Svilanovic, leader of Civil Alliance of Serbia, and Ilic would lead the convoy from Uzice and Cacak; President of Social Democracy Vuk Obradovic and DOS member Jozsef Kasza would lead the convoy from Novi Sad and Subotica; DOS member Dragan Veselinov would be at the head of the Banat convoy, while opposition members Dusan Petrovic and Ratko Filipovic would lead the people of Srem and Sabac.

The DOS leaders had apparently read Curzio Malaparte's *Technique du coup d'état*. When Mussolini set out for Rome in October 1922, wrote Malaparte, nobody could stop him. That was the first part. The second should have been similar to what Trotsky did in October 1917 in St. Petersburg, taking over key points in the city.

The people from Sabac, Srem, and Valjevo were to surround the Belgrade airport; those from Novi Sad the federal government building in New Belgrade; those from Banat the Belgrade police headquarters on 29th November Street. The Nis protesters were to storm the Radio Television Serbia (RTS) building on Takovska Street, and those from Uzice and Cacak were to take the Federal Parliament.

The convoys were equipped with heavy machinery such as bulldozers and trucks as well as weapons and explosives. All possible obstacles had been considered, along with ways to eliminate them.

That's how October 5 was supposed to begin. The people from Nis were to be allowed to do as they pleased at RTS. The task force, with the aid of "insiders" in the Federal Parliament, was to use a ladder to storm the windows, disarm police, and open the doors to Kostunica, the DOS leaders, and hundreds of supporters.

The plan then called for DOS to barricade itself inside the Parliament building with the people outside. They were to call for negotiations on Milosevic's departure while Kostunica addressed the nation.

His speech was to be broadcast by Studio B, already in the hands of Captain Dragan, and then by Television Vracar, whose transmitters had been erected on October 4. This would be followed by TV Pink, an entertainment station whose staff had agreed to take over the station, and finally by RTS itself. A team from the Democratic Party was stationed on Mount Avala where, with special equipment, they would intercept the RTS signal and broadcast the DOS program.

According to the DOS plans, the rest of Serbia was to follow suit. Thousands of demonstrators had been dispatched to block police stations and military barracks. Their orders were not to touch the barracks but to be friendly with the troops. Presents and flowers. Kisses for the boys in uniform.

"That's the way to disarm the military," thought Djindjic on his way back to the party headquarters. He was sleepy and exhausted; he hadn't eaten for four days and had lost nine pounds. When he got back to his office, he pulled the chair up to the desk, stripped down to his underwear, and covered himself with a blanket. What he did next was not so much fall asleep as pass out.

The young Belgrade police officer's face was hardened by fatigue and the job he was doing. "This isn't good," he thought to himself. "It's going to be a hell of a screw up." He closed his eyes. He'd been summoned to the city police headquarters ten hours earlier by Colonel Milos Vojinovic. They'd been there until 11 P.M., making a plan to protect buildings and facilities in the capital. He could see how poor that plan was. Preparations to secure buildings during opposition meetings were normally drawn up by the city police as much as ten days in advance. Who it was that had waited until the eleventh hour, and why, the officer didn't know. He'd been away from Belgrade and Vojinovic had recalled him. At the Belgrade police headquarters he met an official from the Serbian Ministry of Internal Affairs. "If we don't protect these buildings tomorrow we might as well start packing," the panic-stricken man had said.

Nothing else.

He hadn't been given any special orders for the plan. "As if nobody was expecting anything much," the officer thought as he prepared the plan. He couldn't understand it. Not because he had stood for election as a member of the Democratic Party in the early 1990s, but because he was a policeman, and policemen know how the job should be done. "Ten percent of the men with rifles," he thought. "Should I write that down? Nobody asked for them, so I won't. Just batons and chemicals. Nothing else."

He planned two squads for the Federal Parliament, along with those from the Federal Police Brigade, two squads for the Serbian Parliament, two for the president's building, three for RTS, and one for Studio B. Then he added two more. There are 25 men in a police squad. Less than 500 people for all the key buildings in the capital. Added to this were another 600 members of special police units from various Serbian cities (in the end only 300 arrived, from Leskovac, Pirot, and Vranje) and almost 2,500 Belgrade police involved in the events of October 5 in one way or another, either in police stations, at headquarters, or on the outskirts of the city.

Altogether there would be 3,650 police against the protesters.

"Not enough," thought the officer. "A poor estimate."

The police have a tradition of poor estimates, at least as far as demonstrations are concerned. Even in situations such as this, the fear on which the regime was based had taken its toll: Police regularly played down the number of protesters, reporting only a fraction of the number involved. Their reports were read by Milosevic and they feared his anger if he heard the real number, and thus the extent of opposition to his regime.

On the eve of the elections, when Kostunica and Milosevic held rallies at the same time, they had outdone themselves. The police report read that 20,000 people attended Kostunica's rally in front of the Federal Parliament and that 30,000 Milosevic supporters gathered to hear him speak in New Belgrade's sports center.

It was the same on October 5. The last figure quoted on the police radio, at 3 P.M., was 70,000 protesters. Colonel Buha always reckoned on three or four times the official number before going into action. But when he arrived at the back of the Federal Parliament building at about 4 P.M. and saw the demonstrators, he was shocked. "Holy mother," he thought, "there are ten times that many."

The "military commander," Police Minister Vlajko Stojiljkovic, had a hand in the disastrous planning. It was his idea to surround Belgrade with three circles and stop the convoys of demonstrators as soon as they had set out for the capital. The senior police officials hadn't read Malaparte. The revolutionary theoretician says that on days such as October 5 "Trotsky should be confronted by Trotsky." In those terms, the DOS revolutionary committee didn't have a worthy opponent on Serbia's D-day. At the end of the twentieth century, Stojiljkovic's epic military plan, to have one circle wait for those the others let through, seems to have passed its expiration date, to say the least.

More important, this strategy would break the police forces up even before anything had happened. The officers in the green room were very conscious of this. For the first time the special police were to act in small units. They had never been so dispersed before. These units had been established to undertake joint actions. The principle was that men from a number of police divisions would gather in one place rather than chasing protesters at roadblocks in smaller groups.

"It won't work," thought one of the officers, "and nobody has firearms." It was clear to him and everyone else in the room that the whole plan was flawed. They didn't even think of following it.

"After the election, the awareness that Milosevic had lost had sunk into the policemen's minds," said Radomir ("Rade") Markovic, the head of the State Security Service, giving his account for this book. "Whether it was 49-point-something-percent or 50 percent was irrelevant to these people. There was no disputing the fact that Kostunica had won many more votes than Milosevic."

"Kostunica has certainly won," said one of the officers in the room, "I voted for him!"

"The question in the minds of the police was whether to defend that 1 percent or .1 percent," said Markovic.

There were thus two reasons for what happened on October 5: the indecisiveness of the police and the resolve of the demonstrators. Rade Markovic says that the top officials of the state were unaware of either of these.

The State Security Service "knew the plans," he said. "The service was aware of the people's intention to come to Belgrade. It also knew about the leaders. We didn't know, we didn't even dream that they would bring arms. Nobody had thought that the demonstrators were so resolute, so decided, that they were even ready to risk their lives."

Markovic didn't know that his lieutenant, the chief of the Special Operations Units, was meeting Democratic Party President Zoran Djindjic. Nor did he know that, through special lines, the men in the green room were telling the men in the field not to fire. Or that Chief of Staff of the Yugoslav Army Nebojsa Pavkovic was sleeping peacefully because he had already decided not to get his hands dirty the next day.

"I'm not aware of any contact between DOS and the Public Security Service," Markovic said. "I knew there were contacts with the State Security Service, but they were established after the uprising, on the afternoon of October 5, in order to calm the situation down."

According to Markovic, the State Security had "practically nothing to do" until October 5. There are, however, two details that contradict him. The service had probably learned of Djindjic's plan, on the night of September 24, to establish contact between the commander of the anti-terrorist units, Zivko Trajkovic, and Vojislav Kostunica, who had just won the election.

Kostunica and Trajkovic were both for the idea, but it didn't happen. Trajkovic was summarily removed from his position and given a job in Kursumlija, 185 miles from Belgrade. Djindjic became more careful about what he was saying and where, and he used the scrambled satellite telephone more often. State Security also deserves credit for having learned about the truck-load of weapons ordered by Covic. It failed to discover where they arrived, however, and what was unloaded from them.

All in all it was a clumsy business. It was an attempt to stop people who would not be stopped, to fight them with police who no longer wanted to fight for Milosevic, in the belief that only Belgraders would protest in Belgrade and that Belgraders were "nice people who would only sing and dance." This was the thinking of Police Minister Stojiljkovic on the eve of the most significant day in Serbia's recent history.

SEVEN

"ARREST VELJA ILIC AND SVILANOVIC"

A telephone rang in the green room, and one of the officers answered it. It was Ljuba Aleksic, chief of one of the police divisions; Police Minister Sto-jiljkovic's right-hand man.

"Listen, send two squads each from Uzice and Sabac to Mount Rudnik. They have to be there by 6 o'clock."

"Got it," said the officer.

"And that Velja Ilic," continued Aleksic, "and Svilanovic, you know, arrest them and, if possible, have them . . ."

"I couldn't hear that," said the officer.

"It doesn't matter. Arrest them." Aleksic hung up.

Days later, Ceda Jovanovic learned that there had been a plan to assassinate coalition members Goran Svilanovic, leader of Civil Alliance of Serbia, and Velimir "Velja" Ilic, co-president of New Serbia. All he knew that night was that all of them, all the DOS leaders, were targets. And targets were to be eliminated. That's why he was saying to himself "Cedomir, you have to finish the job. You mustn't let them get you."

Others also were concerned for him. Five people came to the Democratic Party headquarters at 1 P.M. "These are your people," said one of the men, waving to the other four. "They have weapons and official identification papers. Where you go, they go."

Ceda set out from the party headquarters with his escorts and a large bag containing two satellite telephones. He needed somewhere safe. A place where they couldn't easily get to him. "In the poorest country in Europe, I decided to begin D-day at the Hyatt Hotel," said Jovanovic, remembering.

The brightly lit Hyatt was full of foreign journalists. There was a shower and a television set in the room. Ceda watched the news from Kolubara. Adrenaline shock. He would need the whole of the next day to bring these dirty, exhausted men in blue overalls to Belgrade. "If only I had a hundred of them," he thought with certainty, "I could break through any cordon and wake Milosevic up." The former leader of student revolutions was shaking like a leaf. He was cold, talking to himself. "Have a bath, Cedomir. You need hot water . . . No, not the bath, you're not a fag, you're a legionnaire, a fighter. The shower, the shower!" A jet of cold water hit him. There was no hot water at the Hyatt on the night of October 4.

Ceda was shivering until morning. Even a swig of whisky from the room's mini-bar couldn't help. It was the first whisky he'd drunk in six or seven months, and it tasted vile. Whisky wasn't the answer. He needed the right people, only that. He needed people who could wake Milosevic up.

Milder, a member of Otpor, the student movement whose name means "resistance," wasn't good at toasts. He didn't even drink; it didn't sit well on his exploding heart. Ten years of personal war with Milosevic. Ten years of constant revolt. The protests of March 9, 1991. The protests on June 28, 1992, St. Vitus Day, one of the most important Serbian holidays, commemorating the Serbian defeat by the Turks in the battle of Kosovo in 1389. He had been sentenced to hard labor for his revolt. He had fought the police. He hated them as much as they hated him.

"Well," Milder said to the party assembled around him in the Zicer Café in the center of Kolarevo, a village near Kraljevo. "Well," he repeated, "those who don't come in the morning . . ." There was no need for any harsher words. They knew what he meant.

At half past one they went on their way. Milder slowly opened the door of his house. His mother was already asleep. "I must leave her something," he thought, "milk, some money . . ." Ever since he'd been beaten by the police in 1996 she hadn't seemed quite all there. He hadn't been broken, but she had.

Milder took his time getting ready. He shaved, showered, pulled on an Otpor T-shirt, packed his things in a bag. "No, no, I mustn't take weapons," he decided. "If I get carried away by the mob, if I get excited, it's better not to have weapons." He needed to be back at the Zicer Café at 6 o'clock. Once everything was ready, Milder slept until 5:15. He dreamt of a revolution. There were buildings on fire.

Sekula saw it this way: "What have you got to lose?" He posed the question to his mates from Kraljevo as they got ready to set off for Belgrade the next morning. "Really, what? Chaos at home, my mother and father both work for twenty Deutschmarks a month, my wife doesn't have a job, my sister doesn't work at all, she needs to get married, her kid's growing up. So let's go, whether we return or not. Wherever the people go, we'll go. We have to do something, whatever might happen to us. That's all I want to say."

"Okay," said Gigo, "Let's go, whatever happens. What do you say, Bubac?"

"Let's do it. Let's get moving."

The buses from Kraljevo were leaving at 6 o'clock from almost right outside Sekula's house. "If you go to sleep you'll be even more tired," Sekula told himself. He kissed his wife and his kid. "See you when I see you." With that he left the house at 4 o'clock. Bubac and Gigo were already in the bus. They'd been first in line.

"Farewell, then," was all Gigo had said to his wife. Bubac hadn't said a word. As preparation for Belgrade, he took a needle, a curved one. He used to be a veterinary technician. "If I can sew up animals, I can do it to myself, no worries," he muttered to Gigo.

These three, Srdjan ("Sekula") Sekulovic, Ivan ("Gigo") Radujevic, and Ljubisa ("Bubac") Milutinovic, would join Milder and thousands of others that day. They would become the army of steel, tough and unstoppable, that Ceda, awake and shivering with cold, had imagined while waiting out the night inside the Hyatt Hotel. They would wake Milosevic up, sweating, as his worst nightmare. They'd pay him back just a fraction of what he'd done to them. He'd transformed these big, upright men into humiliated drifters and losers. But now there was nowhere else to drift, nothing more to lose. They'd hit rock bottom. Now the only way to go was up.

EIGHT

PARLIAMENT WILL BURN

"They've ruined everything for us," Bogoljub ("Maki") Arsenijevic said to himself as he drove back to Borca from the Jojkic Canal, where he had been practicing drills with Molotov cocktails.

He had just driven his "bombers" home to get some sleep. He himself hadn't even thought about sleeping. He was used to getting only two hours a night. And every day he ran 30 miles up and down the Jojkic Canal. Revolution was a serious business for Maki. As was his role in it. "If you want to stand up to them you have to be fit."

"If you want to be fit, don't overburden your stomach," he said as he entered the house. He ate only a little bacon, to raise the low blood pressure which had plagued him for years.

Run, shove, fight barehanded, light fires. These were the things Maki planned to do. And, of course, get killed. He sat at the computer for a while, improvising ambient music to clear his head. Then he read Berdyayev, the Russian philosopher and theologian. The ideas of the philosopher and humanist were not at all brutal in themselves. Yet Berdyayev had foreseen a revolution almost a century earlier.

Maki was thinking about fire. "We only have to light fires. To see the Parliament burning. The symbol of might, the power that has dictated our lives for fifty years. Burn it! Why should it be spared? Everything has been destroyed for us, after all. Let it burn. Let it scare them stiff."

Maki had never had anything to do with military matters, tactics, or strategy. But now he felt that once he had set fire to the Parliament, once Radio Television Serbia (RTS) was ablaze, once the police station on 29th November Street burst into flames, both the police and the army would come to a halt.

"They're scared. When they see flames they're scared. They feel fear just as we do. But they are afraid for their lives, they're frightened of being burned alive, and we are no longer afraid for our lives. Let it burn!"

"That's it," thought Stanko Lazendic, and went to bed. Until a month before he had been one of the most wanted people in Serbia. This Otpor activist, born in Backa Palanka and living now in Novi Sad, knew that if nothing happened in Belgrade on October 5 then there would no longer be a life for him in Serbia. He remembered what the director of federal customs, one of Milosevic's most powerful associates, had written: "Milan Lazendic is dismissed because his brother Stanko Lazendic is a domestic traitor." Signed: Mihalj Kertes.

Stanko had been charged with "inciting murder." The police had found Otpor leaflets in the apartment of Milivoje Gutovic, an unstable character who killed Bosko Perosevic, a senior official of the Socialist Party, on Security Day (the police holiday) on May 13, 2000. The police also had found pamphlets distributed by the Serbian Renewal Movement and other parties. But they alleged that Otpor had incited Gutovic, a man whose mental health was in doubt even before he was arrested, to commit the murder. Stanko Lazendic, as one of the leaders of Otpor, was the first to be accused.

So he had fled to the Bosnian Serb Republic. His brother Milan was fired from his job at TV BAP in Backa Palanka. Mihalj Kertes had decided to dismiss him personally because Backa Palanka was Kertes's hometown, and he liked to keep it under his thumb. Especially as far as "domestic traitor"s were concerned. The charges against Stanko had since been dropped, and the police were polite when he returned to the country on September 15. But it made no difference. "There's no life for me here." Stanko was certain.

"We have to go no matter what happens," he thought. He tried to sleep: He would need all his strength the next day. "We should do it again. The same way we did on the practice runs."

It had taken three days to prepare. Otpor had tested the police. First, at the Varadin Rainbow Bridge in Novi Sad, which had been destroyed by NATO bombs and restored, with great pomp and pride, by Milosevic, they had broken through the police cordon. Then, in front of RTS's Novi Sad premises, they walked through the cordon again.

Each of them knew where they should be positioned, what the task force should be doing, what the rear, armed with stones, should do if the police intervened, how to ensure the safety of the key people, how to communicate, how to use the equipment.

Before he went to sleep, Stanko Lazendic once more ran through the plan for the next day: "Seventeen leaders, each of them with ten people. Rendezvous if the police break us up. Sports gear, socks, a towel, water, a sandwich. Where will Milan be? Where will my uncle be? How long will it take?"

"Five or six days," Stanko told himself as he fell asleep.

"Where are you, my friend?" Sveta Djurdjevic's police contact asked him when Sveta picked up the telephone. Sveta felt better when he heard this. "Where are you, my friend?" was a code. It meant that the senior ranks of the police were finally breaking down and that the police generals were disobeying orders.

Sveta Djurdjevic had been a police officer from 1973 to 1994. He had been head of a police division, a chief inspector, and the commander of a special police unit in Kosovo. He was now with the DOS, in charge of liaison with his former colleagues.

He was also in charge of recruiting determined people from among the ranks of the Democratic Christian Party of Serbia. These were to be on the front line of combat on October 5. They included men from the anti-terrorist units, along with the European and world kick-boxing champions. They'd already arrived in Belgrade from Knjazevac, Obrenovac, from all over Serbia, and were sleeping in the party offices on Zmaja and Nocale Streets, where Djurdjevic was on duty.

He had waited all night for his contact to phone. As he put the receiver down, he smiled. He put on his camouflage jacket, a relic from his old police gear, and set off for home. "I need to shower and shave," he thought. He wanted to be clean and tidy on the road to victory.

Djurdjevic left the party premises. At 5:32 A.M. the DOS electronic surveillance system recorded the first message sent to the police command station, Avala 10, in Belgrade's central police headquarters. It was the chief of police in Cukarica reporting in. "FMP Hall in Zeleznik. DOS is guarding the local radio station."

At 5:40 A.M. Avala 752 told Avala 10, "Operation begun as planned."

Zoran Djindjic woke up at 6 A.M., just as Ceda Jovanovic was leaving the Hyatt. He set off with his people in a white Opel Vectra and a Renault 21. The icy *kosava*, the strong southern wind, was blowing across Belgrade from the plains of inland Serbia. But nobody was quite sure what the weather in Belgrade would be like that day. Instead of a weather forecast, the newspapers already on sale in the streets and kiosks carried a letter from the staff of the Hydro-Meteorological Institute of Serbia. It was concise:

> Because we consider that our wishes and the wishes of most citizens as expressed in the recent presidential election have not been respected, we have decided to express our disagreement in the form of civil disobedience by not issuing weather forecasts to the public. This will continue as long as our wishes are not respected. We ask for your kind understanding.

Politika, the daily newspaper, in what would be its last edition under the control of the Yugoslav Left and Slobodan Milosevic, reported that the Constitutional Court had annulled part of the election proceedings and that the public would be given details later in the day. The Ministry of Foreign Affairs had complained to the UN Security Council about supposed interference from the West in the elections in Yugoslavia. Prime Minister Momir Bulatovic, in an interview broadcast by RTS the previous night, had claimed that Milosevic could remain in office as president until the expiration of his term in June 2001, regardless of whether he won or lost the election.

Information Minister Goran Matic had revealed yet another plot by DOS and foreign powers for the destabilization of the country.

Politika also reported that October 5 was World Day of the Child, that schools were on strike, that some cities were paralyzed, and that power restrictions were in force.

The day's buying rate for the Deutschmark was 36 dinars and the selling rate was 38—normal. The Drivers' Association of Yugoslavia announced that roads were dry and visibility good. Normal. In the day's episode of TV Pink's serial *Rosalinda*, the heroine came to her senses and went out into the street. Everything seemed normal.

Belgrade was packed. People were going to work and shopping, the buses were trundling by, street vendors were opening their stalls. The blockade that had brought the rest of Serbia to a standstill was having little effect in the capital.

This suited Zarko Korac, professor and leader of the Social-Democratic Union. He was sleeping, or rather not sleeping, in his own apartment, despite the warnings. At about 6:30 A.M. he drank a cup of coffee and leafed through the morning newspapers. He was feeling nervous. "This will be an important day in your life, Zarko. You should look smart."

Korac went out for an early walk at 7 o'clock. The crowded streets seemed to be his best refuge. He felt safer among the throngs of people, for the first time in his life. He will remember the paradox as long as he lives: an academic, used to being his own man, was now seeking out busy streets as he walked, staying in the crowds which would protect him if anything should happen. Korac trusted Belgrade. The only thing he feared was that he and the others involved in this dangerous undertaking might let that same Belgrade down. That would be unforgivable.

"We have to take the Parliament," he thought, "and all the other institutions. We simply have to."

Ceda soon cleared his head of the perfumed air of the Hyatt. More than 30 people had been staying night after night in the Democratic Party headquarters, sleeping fully clothed in armchairs and on desks. The air conditioning system was on reverse cycle to keep them warm. "It stinks to high heaven," Ceda thought as he opened the door and entered the lobby of the headquarters building on Proleterskih Brigada Street.

He found Djindjic in his boxer shorts. The party leader's optimism wasn't dampened.

"We'll tear them apart," he said.

"We'll break the motherfuckers," agreed Jovanovic.

Tasks were allocated over coffee. Ceda checked on the convoy leaders. People from Kraljevo had already set out.

"Fucking Serbia!" one man said much later. "This looks like another uprising against the Turkish overlords. Velja's on his way, this one's on his way, that one's on his way. As though all the princes were arriving."

NINE

CACAK ON THE IBAR HIGHWAY

Milder was the first to arrive. Most of the group had assembled in front of the Zicer Café. Some of them were asking angrily, "Why hasn't this one come? Why hasn't that one come?" They swore curtly and then got on the bus. There were no police around Kolarevo. The bus arrived in Kraljevo at 6:15 A.M. The city had long been awake, and the Public Accounting Services building was already surrounded by thousands of people. Again, not a single policeman in sight. "There won't be any bills paid today," thought Milder.

About ten buses and many more cars were parked along Dimitrije Tucovica Street. They were packed with people's belongings: food, drinks, warm clothing. The passengers were waving their cameras like tourists. There would be all sorts of things to photograph in Belgrade.

At 7 A.M. sharp they set off. The people of Kraljevo waved them off from the early-morning coffeehouses. "Stick it to them! Stick it to them!" Milder responded to the encouragement with the Serbian three-fingered salute. He was on the last bus in the convoy.

In the first bus, Sekula, Bubac, and Gigo from Kraljevo were standing between the seats, holding onto straps for balance. All three of them were in their combat gear. Sekula, a judo champion all in blue—blue sweat suit, sneakers, and jacket. There were a number of young girls on the bus. "God only knows what they want out of all this," thought Sekula. At 7:30, in the village of Milocaj, about nine miles from Kraljevo, they ran into the first roadblock.

Fifteen minutes earlier, Avala 10 received a report from the town of Uzice. "Twenty-four buses, one hundred thirty five cars, and one crane have set off." At the same time, the green room at the Ministry of Internal Affairs received information that the special police units had taken up their positions. Everybody in the room knew that no one would fire. "It's better to be humiliated," the colonel said to himself. "Better than civil war."

Goran Svilanovic, the Civil Alliance of Serbia leader, was already up at 5 A.M. "Too early," he thought. He splashed himself with cold water and got dressed. Gray jacket, light blue shirt, gray trousers. No tie. Eleven hours later, still in the same clothes, the cameras would record him entering the Yugoslav Parliament. He arrived at the buses at 6 A.M. "We won't be too late," he thought, as he watched the people of Uzice file hurriedly on board. Uzice had never seen so many people in the streets this early in the morning. Trumpeters in the buses set up a deafening blast. Playing only songs of the Chetniks, filled with nationalism and nostalgia for the guerrillas who had fought the Nazis and the communists in World War II, familiar to all. To boost morale.

At the head of the convoy was a low-loader carrying a bulldozer. Svilanovic got into the bus. The convoy slowly moved off. Svilanovic smiled at the people lining the streets. "Don't come back until you finish the job," they yelled to him. They didn't need to. His wife had said much the same the day before: "Go and get it over with," she told him. The leader of the Civil Alliance had the odd feeling that he'd better not come home without doing as she said.

And now he was looking determined. So was the entire convoy. Some milkmen who had just arrived from Uzice told them that the police had dumped sand into a road tunnel near Lucani, 15 minutes from Uzice. Svilanovic responded by waving his hand. "Let's go!"

"Victory or death!" exclaimed Velja Ilic, DOS leader and co-president of New Serbia, at 6 A.M., at the earliest protest rally ever held in Cacak. "We won't be coming back unless we win!" replied the Cacak protesters. Velja had spent the whole night planning what Djindjic should do, what Kovac should do, where little Daca would be and where Sivac. One thought never left his mind: "How do we wake up Belgrade? If only we can do something on the way to Belgrade, something momentous, then Belgrade will rise up. We'll do it."

Igor, one of the boys from Velja's escort, knew just what to do. His boss had told him: "We'll start a ruckus. Before they do. If we wait for them to start then nothing will happen again. They'll break us up, and everything will be down the drain."

"The shit will hit the fan, boss," said Igor. "It will, don't worry about that." This was his life's mission, to get the better of the cops.

"Take care," his wife had said as he left. "And don't do anything foolish," she added, seeing the look on his face. Velja gave his savings to his neighbor for safekeeping. He kissed each of his five children. But he didn't say a word to his wife. She knew that once he'd decided to do something he'd see it through to the end. Quietly, he left the house.

Zoran Boskovic, a police inspector in Cacak, was Velja's liaison with the anti-terrorist unit of the Serbian police. He had been at the roadblocks near the town of Preljina until 4 A.M. He and his colleague Miladin Milojevic were there to boost the morale of the people and to see whose side the police were on. Once at home, Boskovic fell peacefully asleep.

He awoke after an hour or so. Being a believer, he prayed, "Honestly, we're trying to do the right thing. And if it is the right thing, with God's help we'll succeed." So Boskovic, a policeman and a Kosovo war veteran, collected all the weapons that should be carried by members of the special units. "I'm going to Belgrade," he told his wife. She was astonished.

"You're not going to the demonstrations, are you?"

"They're not demonstrations." It was rebellion speaking through his mouth now. "I'll either come back or stay there."

As he left the house he called on God for help once more. "Wait for me in front of the church," he told his wife, "with the children."

It was an odd convoy that set off from Cacak at 7:15 that morning. There were 230 trucks, 52 buses, and hundreds of cars. Under the tarpaulins of the trucks were Velja's "special troops." Some of them carried crowbars, others had piles of stones. Once the tarpaulins were lifted the bombing could begin. Still more "special troops" were in cars.

In one car alone there were a carbine with telescopic sights and 200 rounds, a sawed-off Zastava shotgun, a TT 7.62 mm rifle, a 7.65 mm Zastava rifle, and a Scorpion with a silencer and eight mortars. In another car there was a fighter with a hunting rifle, two pistols, a bayonet, a helmet, and a flak jacket. The Kalashnikovs—submachine guns—and the Wasps—rocket launchers—were hidden.

This was heavy traffic for the Ibar Highway. When the head of the convoy reached the Milanovac dairy, its tail was just leaving Preljina, 14 miles behind.

Near Majdan, about six miles past Gornji Milanovac, where the road begins to climb the foothills of Mount Rudnik, the Cacak team hit its first roadblock.

"Today's the day," Otpor activist and "domestic traitor" Stanko Lazendic told himself. His wristwatch said 7 A.M. He was out of bed on time. There were good-byes to be said before he left for Belgrade. "All I've been doing lately is saying goodbye and going somewhere else," he thought. As he drank his morning coffee at his office, the city of Novi Sad's civil engineering inspectorate, his co-workers asked him what he thought was going to happen in Belgrade. Then they embraced and he said goodbye.

There were 25 buses parked in Novi Sad's central square. He got into the first one. The president of Social Democracy, Vuk Obradovic, was leading the convoy. He was already on the bus. So were Milan, Stanko's brother, and his uncle. The uncle was no rookie: he had been at Vukovar as a reserve soldier. "Forget your singing and dancing this time," he told Stanko. "We need to do something concrete."

The convoy set off at 9 A.M. Novi Sad was ringing with Serbian marching songs, Chetnik ones, and the familiar chant of "Kill yourself and save Serbia, Slobodan." The first roadblock was right outside Novi Sad, at the motorway junction. A dozen police officers in ordinary uniforms were there. They had put red and white plastic road-marking cones across the road. "It'll be a roadblock when it grows up," Stanko joked to his uncle.

Obradovic got out to negotiate.

"The road is closed," a policeman explained, "you can't go through."

The words were hardly out of his mouth before Stanko was out of the bus, picking up the road cones.

"They're ours, leave them alone," said a man in uniform, grabbing him by the arm.

"What's yours?" roared the Otpor leader. "Is the road yours? What else is yours?"

By now they were all out of the bus, Milan, the uncle, and a mob of young men. They grabbed the police by the shoulders and dragged them from the road.

"You could have told us you wanted to get through," one of them grumbled.

There was no stopping the Novi Sad convoy now. The adrenaline was flooding through them. More than 200 vehicles joined them along the way. A few police near the outer Belgrade suburb of Batajnica waved "Stop, stop!" and then quickly got out of the way. The buses trundled on. On to Belgrade. The Otpor battalion.

"Look how strong we are!" Stanko shouted to his uncle. "Very, very strong!"

Thirty-odd police, with flak jackets and riot shields, stood outside the town of Milocaj, a police truck and a fire engine blocking the road in front of them. The first bus from Kraljevo stopped about fifty yards away. Milder ran up from the last bus. Sekula, Gigo, and Bubac already stood facing the cordon. "Pesic, move the police away!" shouted Milder. "Move them away! If somebody gets hurt you'll be to blame!"

Pesic, the commander of the Kraljevo police, was one of the few familiar faces among the officers at the roadblock. The majority weren't locals. "You're from Pozarevac!" the people behind Milder were shouting. "From Kosovo!" Stones were hurled at the police.

It didn't take long before Sekula asked, "Why are we asking them to move? Why ask? We won't get anywhere if we start asking. Get moving, get into the truck."

Radisa, one of Milder's lecturers from his days at teacher-training college, jumped into the truck and put it into gear. Another moved the fire engine. Now only the police themselves blocked the way. "Push, push!" cried the mob. They leaned into the police shields. Everyone against the cordon. First the people, then the buses. The police moved aside.

But Milder wasn't satisfied. "Too slow," he thought. "When will we get to Belgrade?" The others in the last bus, the Zicer Café crowd, felt the same way. "Step on it, chief," Milder told the driver. The man leaned on the horn and moved into the fast lane. All the way to Belgrade Milder called to people waving from their balconies, "Come with us, what are you waiting for?" The bus from Kolarevo eventually overtook even the Cacak crew and was the first to pull up outside the Parliament.

The police officers lined up in front of the tunnel near the town of Lucani didn't look frightening at all. Goran Svilanovic, part of the Uzice convoy, looked them over carefully but couldn't see any weapons. There were about 30 of them, including a commander.

"There's sand blocking the tunnel," the commander told Svilanovic.

"Okay," said the Civil Alliance leader. "We'll take care of that straightaway."

The police commander didn't say another word. Only Svilanovic spoke. To his people first of all: "Unload the bulldozer."

Then he turned back to the commander. "You'd better get out of the way. My people can hardly wait to see you standing in front of them. Better move your men away."

The commander obeyed without a word.

It took the bulldozer less than ten minutes to clear the sand. The caravan sped through the tunnel. At the other end they found about 50 police, with Black Marias and jeeps, standing beside the road.

This time the police commander addressed Svilanovic calmly, reciting, as though reading a formal report to his superiors: "We've done what we were required to do. We put the cordon in place. The opposition was stronger. We had to withdraw."

Svilanovic sped on to Belgrade. Right behind Velja Ilic in the Cacak convoy.

In the green room a telephone rang. The colonel picked up the receiver. "All right," he said.

He rang headquarters on another line. "Our men put the cordon in place. The opposition was stronger. They had to withdraw."

Much later, recounting the events for this book, the colonel said: "No roadblock can work if you don't have men who will defend it, men who are prepared to fire. We knew that they'd all get to Belgrade."

At the town of Majdan there was a truck, a trailer, and a Black Maria blocking the road. About 40 police stood along the side. Their gear—flak jackets, shields, and helmets—hung on trees nearby. The police were smoking, some of them leaning on their shields.

Velja and his men drove through the roadblock and stopped near the policemen.

"You'll have to wait for the chief," said the commander.

"Which do you like more, your job or your life?" asked Velja's bodyguard, Igor.

"They're frightened," said Velja, looking at the boyish faces of the policemen.

Behind them, the truck and the Black Maria were being thrown around like tin cans. The men from Cacak pushed them into the ditch with their bare hands.

"They're getting wild," Velja told the officer. "You're annoying them."

The officer didn't say a word.

Thousands of people from Cacak were rushing toward the police with sledgehammers, crowbars, hammers, and clubs. The officer turned to where his men had been. They were already fleeing for the nearby woods.

"Like a tornado," thought Velja, more cheerful now, satisfied with the tried-and-true formula: a mob of angry men against the roadblocks.

"No one will stop us."

Democratic Christian Party leader Vladan Batic awoke at 7 A.M. He prayed and said goodbye to his wife and children. Then he phoned Velja Ilic.

"Everything's in place, are you coming?" he shouted from Obrenovac.

"We're coming, brother, we're coming," replied Velja from somewhere on the road. "We're breaking their balls, it's like taking candy from a baby."

"Well done," said Batic. "Well done, Velja."

Three days earlier, on the night of October 1, Batic's mother had died. His father hadn't lived to see the new Serbia, either. Batic had placed an obituary in the daily *Glas javnosti*: "Mother, tell Dad that we've won." Now, hearing Velja, he knew he hadn't lied.

"Thank God," he was thinking, while Velja was still shouting down the line: "Hey, are the Delije ready?" He wanted to make sure the dedicated and resolute fans of the Red Star soccer team were on board.

"Everything's ready, Velja. Just keep going, their people are waiting for you near [the town of] Ljig."

"We'll crush them, it's child's play!" Velja Ilic shouted into the telephone. He was already approaching the town of Celije, speeding ahead at the front of the convoy that had now spread across both lanes of the Ibar Highway. The road was theirs alone.

After they passed Ljig they ran into a new roadblock near the mill at the town of Lajkovac. The highway there passes between a few houses. On top of a hill to the right is a church with a tall steeple. Leading down the hill is a track that the local farmers use to drive their tractors and trailers onto the highway. To the left is a large industrial mill. Also on the left are the railway line from Lajkovac and the exit from the highway to Struganik.

There were three trucks, one of them a tanker, and a police four-wheel drive parked across the road a short distance before the exit overpass to the mill. About 150 policemen were standing some 50 yards behind on both sides of the road. They were in full gear and carrying weapons, including tear-gas guns. In the distance, near the Struganik exit, an armored personnel carrier was parked in the middle of the road with rubber shielding on the wheels and a machine gun on top.

"About 30 of us," Velja's bodyguard Igor estimated when he saw the personnel carrier. "That's how many of us will get killed in the first wave. The rest will get through." He set off in the front line for the roadblock.

He ran to a man standing next to the tanker. "They forced me, they forced me!" the man cried in fear.

"Who could force you to park your tanker here? Who, you motherfucker?" Igor roared. He punched him. Some of the others laid into him, too. Fury isn't pretty, even when it's revolutionary fury. The tanker driver was screaming.

Meanwhile, Velja was trying to get through more politely. About 50 yards farther on he approached the first of the policemen: "Move these things away please, sir. We've broken through everything on our way. Don't force us to smash these up."

The men from Cacak were already unloading the bulldozer.

The policeman panicked. He raised his baton. Velja winced.

The rubber baton, whistling as it fell, grazed the arm he lifted at the last moment and caught him on the shoulder blade.

"Fuck you!" screamed Velja.

The tanker driver, curled up on the asphalt, stopped screaming. He was no longer surrounded by the mob of angry men. They were already running, fists clenched, toward the police officer, Igor in the lead again. Behind them, the whole of Cacak was roaring.

The man in the blue uniform tried to reach the highway. They caught him near the shoulder of the road. He threw his arm above his head and tried to say, "Don't!"

"He hit me without warning!" Velja told someone on the telephone later. "And so they beat the shit out of him."

The other police ran. The trucks and the tanker were shoved aside. Again by hand. The armored personnel carrier drove off by itself.

"There's no going back now," said Igor with certainty as he watched the convoy speed on. Everything was clear to him now. He had seen the camera crews recording them tearing apart the police and the roadblocks, and he had seen the police jeep drive off toward Belgrade with the tape.

"Three to fifteen years of hard labor for hitting him," he told himself. "That's the law." Then he threw his hands in the air: "As if I cared!"

There was no way he could go home. Not if he didn't succeed in Belgrade. He could only take to the woods. Nowhere else to go.

"Fuck it," he said. He was thinking about his wife and kid. They lived off the profits of his small business, wheeling and dealing, black marketeering. "It has to succeed," he said, stepping on the gas. Nobody tried to stop them again, the rest of the way to Belgrade. Driving through the Lipovica woods, the police didn't even dare show themselves on the road. They hid behind the trees and watched the convoy drive past.

Giving his account for this book, Velja spoke about his fellow citizens from Cacak: "I was shouting 'Stop! Stop for a minute!' to slow them down a little, but it was no use. I couldn't stop them. They simply breezed through."

They left a trail like a hurricane. Svilanovic and the people of Uzice, Milder and the others from Kraljevo, Zoran Boskovic, whom Velja had left at the rear of the convoy—all saw the same scattered police squads, disheveled policemen huddled in groups, trucks in the roadside ditches, here and there a police car or an ambulance overturned. Some of the police waved to them, saluting the buses, which blew their horns as they passed.

The special police units had been dispersed, somewhat to their relief, and wouldn't be brought back together again that day.

Head of State Security Rade Markovic described it as another in a series of errors by the police: "The units manning the roadblocks should have been rounded up and brought to Belgrade on the back roads. That didn't happen."

Only the commanders of some of the units made it to the capital. They arrived in the green room.

"It's all over," they said. The colonel was satisfied.

TEN

GLORIJA AT THE GENERAL STAFF

On the first floor of the Belgrade police headquarters at 29th November Street there is a large room with video monitors showing what police cameras in Belgrade's main streets are recording. At 8 A.M. on October 5, information was received on the first gathering of citizens, near the Belgrade railway station in front of the Belgrade University economics department.

At 8:20, Avala 10 received reports that the people had reached Republic Square. At 9 A.M. came the information that the protestors had used roadside garbage containers to block streets in the outer Belgrade suburb of Vozdovac.

A little earlier, at about 7:15, the police officer who had planned the protection of Belgrade's key buildings the night before was driving to work. Behind him was a convoy of cars with DOS flags in New Belgrade, and he slowed down to let them pass.

"I'm in no hurry today," he thought. His blue police car was stuck behind the fifth or sixth vehicle of the DOS convoy. They crawled slowly to Branko's Bridge, the busiest traffic artery across the Sava River. There are three bridges across the Sava, but almost a million people from New Belgrade, Zemun, and the suburbs sprawling along the nine-mile stretch to the airport use this bridge to reach the bustling and congested center of Belgrade.

Some time after 8 A.M. the bridge was blocked. The blue police car was in the middle of the blockade. The man in uniform who got out of the car was smiling.

This was only one of many roadblocks in Belgrade, part of DOS's strategy to defend the occupied center of Belgrade, should their plan succeed. The opposition coalition's activists had made plans to block all traffic routes through which military and police reinforcements could reach the city center, the

Parliament, and Radio Television Serbia (RTS). One was Kneza Milosa Street, which would be used by troops from the Banjica barracks and the First Armored Brigade. They also blocked the Zagreb Motorway and all three bridges on the Sava, thus cutting off the center from any attack that might come from the other side of the river. The Danube bridge was cut off, isolating the military police based in the suburb of Pancevo. The other blockades were on Srpskih Vladara Street, which runs past the large square in front of the Yugoslav Parliament, and Revolution Boulevard, the city's longest street, which leads to the suburbs on the banks of the Danube.

Anything large and on wheels was pressed into service for the blockades. Cars, garbage containers, the City Transport Company's buses and trams, water tankers belonging to the city's parks and gardens department, garbage trucks, machinery from the city roadworks division. The city authorities, who were under the control of the Serbian Renewal Movement until October 5, had no interest in preventing the requisition of all this equipment. In any case, they couldn't have: DOS already had a grip on the city's public service depots and garages. DOS local branches in Belgrade's boroughs blocked the streets and squares in their own areas. This was yet another ring of security around the center of the city, more efficient than those that the poorly informed Police Minister Stojiljkovic had tried to set up.

If necessary, the city center would be virtually inaccessible during the afternoon and evening of October 5. The roadblocks, unlike those on the Ibar and other highways guarded by police, were guarded by people who were determined to fire—and to fire whatever was needed to stop whatever needed stopping. Wasps—hand-held rocket launchers—were on standby to protect against tanks.

General Nebojsa Pavkovic, chief of staff of the Army, wasn't much worried about all this. His day, like any other, began in military fashion. He rose at 6:30 A.M. and was at work at the Yugoslav Army General Staff Headquarters on Neznanog Junaka Street by 7:15. Pavkovic was one of a select few who were privy to a most significant piece of information: There were very few soldiers in Belgrade that day. They'd been withdrawn and transferred to other barracks days earlier. From the early morning, the army didn't want to interfere. Later, Pavkovic said that the only thing that concerned him was the news, by now a day old, that the government might be preparing a counter-demonstration. Army intelligence had learned that the Left was also making plans for a rally in Belgrade on October 5.

The Sixty-Third Paratroop Brigade, from Nis, had been deployed around the General Staff Headquarters. This special unit was well known to Belgraders. During the opposition protests in 1996 and 1997, Vuk Draskovic, the president of the Serbian Renewal Movement, had read a letter of support from the brigade to thousands of Belgraders from a window in Terazije Square.

Pavkovic took care of his own safety without the knowledge of either Milosevic or the police. His wife, Glorija, and their children were with him in the headquarters that day. "They stayed all day. They even slept there that night," said Pavkovic, showing a room adjacent to his large office. "Just in case."

Pavkovic immediately put the General Staff on alert. The 13 generals who made up the Supreme Command Committee together watched what was happening on the streets of Belgrade and on the access roads to the capital.

As early as 9 A.M. it was clear to the army's leadership that the police were not doing what they were supposed to do. There were virtually no roadblocks, at least not in any form that would prevent the demonstrators from coming to Belgrade. The generals were listening in on police communications in addition to receiving information from the military counterintelligence service. This was to be of great significance later in the day. When the police asked the army to step in, claiming that people had been killed at Radio Television Serbia, Pavkovic was able to tell them confidently: "No one is dead."

A few hundred yards from the General Staff building, in the Banjica neighborhood, is the headquarters of the State Security Service, next door to the Military Medical Center. On the morning of October 5, the courtyard of the Institute for Security was filled with secret police playing soccer. The members of the State Security Special Operations Unit, the "Boys from Brazil," as police radio referred to them later in the day, were not in the least bit nervous as they kicked the ball around. The Special Operations Commander was also playing. He had earlier put the units on a low-level alert.

Meanwhile, the first convoys of angry demonstrators were breaking through the fragile roadblocks and rushing, sparks flying, headlong for Belgrade. At about the same time one of the officers in the green room calmly went home to sleep. The police and military clearly thought the story was over. Milosevic, as yet, didn't have a clue that the police would not carry out his orders.

ELEVEN

MUTINY AT THE BASTILLE

The casual observer could have been forgiven for thinking that everything was normal in Belgrade that morning. The city looked as it always did, perhaps only a little bit calmer, a little bit quieter. The icy *kosava*, the strong southern wind, was blowing across the city, but the real storm was still miles away, venting its fury on the police roadblocks.

At this hour, the people in charge of October 5 in Belgrade were still invisible. They could sense the tempest; they expected it and, coordinated or not, were doing all they could to prepare for the day. Several non-government organizations (NGOs)—the Yugoslav Committee of Lawyers, the Humanitarian Law Center, the Peace and Crisis Management Foundation, and the Civil Initiative—agreed to collect data on everyone detained by the regime in the previous ten days, during the blockades and protests in Belgrade. They did this without publishing the names of the people arrested or the prisons in which they were being held.

By 10 A.M. these organizations had their members in Masarikova Street, in front of the City Magistrate's Court. This institution was notorious for dispensing summary justice to protesters and for its rigorous enforcement of the Public Information Act. Under this legislation, introduced in October 1998, journalists were treated in the same way as petty thieves and prostitutes, with the difference that they were subject to much tougher fines. The anti-journalism legislation raised a total of 2,501,737 Deutschmarks, or $1,137,153, for the state's coffers. This, according to Milosevic and his court, was the price of "public disturbance, libeling senior officials, and undermining the constitutional order and the government"—the crimes most frequently cited in the court's long-winded rulings.

Rade Veljanovski, Biljana Kovacevic-Vuco, Natasa Kandic, Miljenko Dereta, Gradimir Nalic, and the other NGO members made their way to the City Magistrates Court in pairs, to avoid attracting the attention of the security guards. The court's president, Dobrivoje Glavonjic, was as notorious as the bench he presided over.

Glavonjic wasn't looking at all himself on the morning of October 5. "Give them the lists," he said, smiling at his secretary. "The lists of the people who have been arrested." The NGO representatives were astounded to hear him promise, "Believe me, from now on, whenever anyone is detained we shall notify their families and you immediately." So even the regime's most loyal supporters no longer believed it would survive. The establishment, servile and frightened, had realized that its leader had no future.

This was apparent at every level, from the top to the bottom. The security guards at the Magistrates Court were, unbelievably, smiling. They were pleased at the success of the NGO deputation. Only then did the NGO members realize that their charade of entering the building in pairs had been unnecessary. Everybody in the court knew who they were and what they were there for. The spirit of revolution was spreading infectiously throughout the city.

NGO member Rade Veljanovski, a former Radio Belgrade editor in chief, was overjoyed. The day had already begun well, and he had his own plans. "I have to be part of it," he had decided at 7:30 that morning, as soon as he opened his eyes. He knew what was going to happen. He had felt it and had seen it in Serbia long before September 24, when he had toured 40 Serbian cities in as many days with the non-partisan Exit 2000 campaign.

"They can put up whatever barriers they like," he said, remembering the energy that he had seen sweeping through Serbia. "They'll come. The people of Cacak, Novi Sad, Uzice, all of them."

The meeting with Glavonjic had given him even more confidence. Veljanovski, who would later that day play a role in the conquest of the television center and Radio Belgrade, hurried to his office. He had to listen to the news and then rush to the Independence Trade Unions. That was where the radio and television strikers were heading.

Juliana Jovanovic, the assistant editor in chief of Radio Television Serbia's current affairs programming, wasn't aware of any of these events when she awoke at 6:30 A.M. As she drank her coffee, the last thing on her mind was the demonstrations. She had worked for RTS for most of the past ten years, apart from a period as an assistant to Serbia's minister for information. She had been a member of the Socialist Party from the beginning. "There's always some demonstration or the other," she thought. She was used to them. Sometime before 10 A.M. she set off for work, still unaware of what was happening. She knew nothing of the roadblocks or Velja's breakthrough. Nor did she know that her colleagues at the state media had called a strike. It was just like any other day. Ordinary.

Juliana entered the television center through the main entrance on Takovska Street. She passed through the broad entrance hall without seeing a single police officer. There were not even any extra guards. Next to a booth marked "Security," she inserted her card in a slot and squeezed through the electronic turnstile. Then she took the elevator to the third floor and entered her office. As she arrived at her desk, Juliana was confident that everything was completely normal.

"I didn't go out!" an agitated journalist said to her, half an hour later.

"Out where?" she asked.

"They said that I was with the strikers," the journalist explained. Discipline was a serious matter at RTS.

"What strikers?" asked Juliana.

This was the first she heard about what was happening in Belgrade that day. Sometime later, watching videotapes with editors Zeljko Avramaovic and Sasa Barbulovic, she saw a whole cross section of the RTS staff—journalists, camera crew, directors, and technicians—standing in a park just across Aberdareva Street and the television building, waving and shouting.

The chief engineer of RTS technical services, Radisa Petrovic, had arrived from Australia the night before. After a month of non-stop work and a 36-hour flight to Belgrade, he hadn't even had time to relax with his wife and child before the telephone rang. It was Milan Topalovic, the technical director of RTS: "Straight to work in the morning. Or else . . ."

"That's enough," Radisa replied. It didn't even cross his mind to go to work. It wasn't because he was exhausted from his month leading the state media's team coverage of the Olympic games, nor because of his jet lag. It wasn't fatigue he was feeling, it was what he had already heard about in Sydney. He felt rebellion.

The RTS staff already had a name for it: general strike. Radisa, who had worn out his shoes during the protests of 1996 and 1997, knew that the situation was different this time. He left his house that morning in much the same way as he had when leaving for Australia before. He left instructions for his wife: "This is here, that's there. In case I don't come back."

Radisa had already made a decision. "I'll lose my job; they may even do worse to me, but it's worth it." As he traveled to the central business district from Residential Block 70 in New Belgrade, the gray dormitory suburb across the Sava River, he thought about the way ahead in the rebellion. Above all he thought about his future and that of his 18-month-old child back at his apartment.

By 8:30 he was already at the Lasta bistro on the edge of Tasmajdan Park, a few hundred yards from the RTS building on Takovska Street. This had been the usual haunt of the company's technical crew since they had gathered there on April 29, 1999, the day after 16 of their co-workers were killed by NATO bombs. From that day, all major technical decisions had been made at the Lasta bistro.

From the Lasta he could see his striking colleagues from other divisions of the state broadcaster assembling about twenty yards away from the entrance to the RTS building, in front of the Dusko Radovic Theatre. Nearby stood a small monument to the 16 workers killed in the bombing. It had been paid for by their parents and families, with no contribution whatsoever from RTS management.

He heard whistling, a highly effective form of reproach and censure, and looked over to see what was going on. The target: The senior executives of RTS who were getting out of an expensive black car in the parking lot off Aberdareva Street. About 20 seconds later the whistling stopped, as the company's director-general, Dragoljub Milanovic, disappeared into the RTS doorway. Later that day, he would run out the same door, straight into the clenched fists of angry demonstrators.

Half an hour later a nervous RTS clerk approached Radisa. "I have to tell you something," she whispered. "I've just typed your dismissal notice."

"That's the least I expected," replied Radisa. "It's okay."

Strikers marched past the television building, onto Majke Jevrosime Street and then onto Nusiceva Street and the headquarters of the Independence Trade Unions. A few women were staring arrogantly out from behind the RTS curtains, making obscene gestures to show their contempt for the strikers.

"Black out the picture!" The idea flashed into Miodrag Zupanc's head in the middle of the night after he asked himself, "What now?" The RTS strike committee had been set up the day before. He had joined the committee and in this way kissed goodbye to his position as editor of school programs. The general strike would begin the morning of October 5. Neither Zupanc nor any of his fellow employees had any idea what form the strike should take. "Should we walk out of the building?" he wondered. "And who should go? Journalists and technicians?"

At the Independence Trade Union offices at 11 A.M., the strike committee was still trying to get its act together. People were tossing ideas around; everybody had something different in mind. Then somebody, Zupanc doesn't remember who it was, shouted, "Listen, we've got to pull the plug!" That was it! The strike committee decided to close down the broadcast. The technical staff had it in their power to cut transmission.

TWELVE

BULLDOZER!

"Bye-bye, Beirut," said Slobodan Ivanovic. He sat up in bed. It was exactly 6 A.M. A trip to Beirut to celebrate his 30 years of marriage was going down the drain that October 5. Ivanovic looked at the air tickets on his bedside table. "It's going to be Bucharest all over again here," he shivered. The comparison to the bloody revolution that had overthrown Romanian dictator Ceausescu and his wife, who were killed, seemed pretty sound. He hadn't slept much that night. Where should he deploy his teams? What would actually happen? Had they packed breathing tubes for cases of suffocation? Bandages? "There must be a field hospital," he thought.

Ivanovic is and was the director of the Anlave Clinic. The "streetwalker," as he affectionately calls it, has had its mobile teams at every demonstration in Belgrade since 1996. Ivanovic had seen combat at close hand as a war surgeon, and many of the things he had seen had not been pretty sights.

He didn't feel himself as he got up that morning. Nor had he felt himself when he went to bed the night before, already dreading what everyone at the clinic was calling D-day. He had seven mobile units prepared, with specialists in anesthetics, surgery, and internal medicine, backed up by fifth- and sixth-year medical students. He ran through the litany of locations: "the central post office, Yugoslav Airlines, Hotel Ekscelzior, the Slovenijasport store, the Borba building, and the field hospital. Twenty-two people. I suppose it will be enough."

He had planned to set up the field hospital in Pioneer Park, facing the Federal Parliament. He was there before 9 A.M. The Democratic Opposition of Serbia, DOS, had erected a metal fence around it, protection in case of a stampede. The anesthetists and surgeons arrived with their equipment. "It will be fine," said Ivanovic. And then he saw them.

Two young men, no more than 18 years of age, freshly graduated from the police secondary school.

"Doctor, you are ordered to pack up your hospital and move away."

"Move where?" Ivanovic was dumbfounded.

The boys in blue shrugged.

Ivanovic tried to stall. He called Branko Stojadinovic, commander of Stari Grad police station. He was given 20 minutes to leave. If he failed to comply, his equipment would be impounded. He left. That evening, as he watched the same Stari Grad police station burn, he remembered the commander shouting into the telephone: "There won't be any rally, Doctor, not in front of the Parliament. It will be in Republic Square. Get out of that park!" Ivanovic couldn't believe his ears. "Either I'm mad or this man doesn't have a clue."

He did set up his field hospital in the end, early in the afternoon, after the first clash between police and demonstrators, pitching his white tent with its red cross in nearby Nikola Pasic Square. The police didn't come near him.

Stojadinovic could hardly be blamed for his ignorance. The police were perplexed by the hundreds of activities going on around Belgrade that day. Everybody—DOS, the NGOs, and all the other groups who were serious about October 5—was doing something: stopping traffic, marching, closing shops, or assembling groups of people in various squares. This even succeeded in confusing the police radio communications. The police command station Avala 10 in the Belgrade police station, under the direct command of the Ministry of Internal Affairs, didn't even have time to log all the calls it received from its field units.

On top of that there was Velja Ilic, along with those in the other convoys, heading for Belgrade. Police no longer knew who was doing what or where. A convoy near the town of Lazarevac was reported to Avala 10 at 10 A.M., and one near Barajevo immediately after that; at 10:53, one in Rusanj; at 11, in Lipovica; at the same time another strike was reported in Belgrade, in front of the critically important Politika building. Another convoy was spotted near Mladenovac at 11—ten buses and four freight trucks; a minute later protesters attacked a traffic patrol in Kneza Milosa Street; in Republic Square somebody was setting up a dais; at 11:15 people began to gather in Pozeska Street in the suburb of Banovo Brdo; at 11:20 the convoy from Lipovica reached Kneza Milosa Street; at 11:43 a two mile–long convoy was reported coming from Zeleznik; at 11:44 a bulldozer, two freight trucks, and about fifty pedestrians on foot blocked traffic near the Federal Parliament. How could anyone cope with all that? Maybe Trotsky, who, as he prepared for the October Revolution, had said: "Chaos is good for revolution. Disorder is my ally."

Such thoughts were far from restaurant worker Ivan Nikolic's mind. Sometime after 10 A.M. he was walking on the Old Obrenovac Road. He walked more than a mile every day along the deserted road winding along Ada Ciganlija and the Sava Lake, the city's largest river beach, to the Lovacka Prica restaurant where he worked. But now the road was packed. "Fucking hell," said Ivan to himself. There were thousands of people in hundreds of trucks, cars, buses, and more trucks. Ivan's walk to work takes him about 15 minutes. For the whole of that time they kept passing, blowing horns, raising their fists, and they were still passing even after he arrived at the restaurant.

Ivan turned around. He was a member of Delije, the aggressive tribe of Red Star soccer fans. He had two court convictions for fighting with police and was one of the guys who chanted "Kill yourself and save Serbia, Slobodan," at the matches. He wasn't going to miss an event like this.

He took out his cell phone and called Marko, his mate.

"Hey, man, you should see what's going on here!" he said.

Marko called the rest of the Delije crew. They agreed to meet at McDonald's in Terazije Square at noon.

"Belgrade!" cried Igor. The people of Cacak descended on Belgrade. As they drove through the suburbs of the city, people were throwing flowers at them, waving from bus stops, from windows. "Go for it!" they were shouting. This irritated Igor. "Why aren't they joining us straightaway?" he wondered. Near the Sava Lake they sped past a guy who was watching them with astonishment. "What's up with him?" Igor asked himself.

They didn't stop. Straight to the railway station, then up Nemanjina Street and past the bombed-out former Yugoslav Army General Staff building along Kneza Milosa Street. They ignored red lights: They were in a hurry. An angry traffic officer stopped Velja's car. He slapped the car: "What are you doing, going through red lights?" Igor punched him, and the policeman's cap fell. Velja and his men stepped on the gas. Straight ahead to the Parliament. It was 11:30 A.M. precisely. Avala 10 received a report of an attack on a traffic patrol on Kneza Milosa Street.

Two minutes later, the police headquarters heard about people gathering on Pozeska Street. The police reports still hadn't mentioned what would turn out to be the most important word of the day: "Bulldozer." But the bulldozer was there.

An International 538, American, no special nickname. Earthmover, front-end loader, bulldozer: it was all the same to Joe. He had wanted to have it decorated. He stopped in front of a Gorica supermarket near the Democratic Party branch in Banovo Brdo. "Decorate it!" he said and blew the horn. The bulldozer joined the whistlers. The protesters plastered it with stickers spelling out the most important pre- and post-election slogan in Serbia: "He's finished." Everyone knew that "he" was Milosevic.

Decorated, the bulldozer took its place at the head of the convoy. And then Joe saw the dog. It wasn't big, but it was biggish. A spotted dog, a perfect specimen of the local strays. Belgrade's stray dogs are a special kind, with a reputation for following protest marches and barking at policemen. Not a day of the three-month 1996–1997 protests passed without strays in attendance. These four-legged vagabonds were the noisy mascots of the demonstrations and have given rise to the legend of the tough Belgrade dog. "This is a good-luck sign," thought Joe. The dog stood on the front of the bulldozer, not moving, all the way to the Parliament before running away, barking, into the angry mob.

Joe fired up the engine. "Stop!" cried an old man. Milan Katic, a 72-year-old local baker, wanted to go and "conquer the Parliament." So Joe gave him a lift. As the convoy set off from Pozeska Street, nobody could have dreamt that this old man and the crippled bulldozer driver, whose spine had been broken in childhood, were about to topple the notorious TV Bastille.

THIRTEEN

THE PATRIARCH'S BLESSING

People were pouring into Belgrade. The students had left their dorms and were on their way to the center of the city. Ceda Jovanovic's scouts were checking whether everything was clear beyond the bridge, the breaking point of demonstrations in previous years. "Don't cross if there are police there," ordered Ceda, who was experienced in these affairs. "They'll throw you into the river."

In the center of the city, members of G17 Plus, the NGO tied to DOS, were building a stage in Republic Square. For a while, the Belgrade police believed that this would be the rallying point, rather than the Parliament.

The confusion hadn't been deliberately created. Mladjan Dinkic, the executive director of G17 Plus, had called a rally in the square for quite a different reason. He wanted people to march through the main streets of downtown to the First Municipal Court, on Slobodana Penezica Krcuna Street, to file criminal complaints—30 pages of them—against the Federal Election Commission and Slobodan Milosevic.

In the DOS plan, Djindjic's people and the students were to wake Belgrade up, making a noise to attract people to the square in front of the Federal Parliament.

It was about then, sometime before noon, that popular initiative began to reshape the plan devised by the DOS leaders in late September at Nebojsa Covic's factory, in the dark room reeking of the kitchen. Something quite different from what the three DOS leaders had cooked up was about to happen in Belgrade.

"What did you dream?" Nenad Ristic's wife asked him. He had been sacked from Radio Television Serbia (RTS) the day before. In Retenzije, the area of

New Belgrade where they lived, the day was already noisy. For four days one of their neighbors had been playing Radio Indeks, the rebellious student radio, at full volume through speakers placed in his windows. Mrs. Ristic liked to interpret dreams. There couldn't have been a better time to test her skill. Everybody knew that something would happen on October 5. She wanted to know more.

"Don't go," she said when Nenad told her he had dreamt about his hometown of Veliko Laole. In the dream, his school friend's son had found him there; they quarreled and the boy beat him. "After that I wandered through the village looking for my school friend, but I didn't find him," Nenad said.

"They'll beat you today," said his wife. "Don't go!"

Nenad laughed.

Hours later, when tear-gas canisters were hurled from the Parliament, Nenad would be dazed and really become lost. He wouldn't be beaten, but the dream was not so far from reality: Ristic had been the director of RTS and on October 5 the RTS director was beaten, although it was his replacement, the new director, Dragoljub Milanovic. Ristic hadn't dreamed about the burning of the Parliament, the television center, or the police center.

A pall of smoke had hung over Belgrade from early in the morning. One burly fireman, setting off on foot at 6 A.M. to his fire station near the New Cemetery, saw burning garbage containers along the way.

"All of them were on fire," he later told the other firemen. "In Kralja Petra Street, in Cara Dusana Street, Skenderbegova and Visokog Stevana Streets, everywhere!"

Everyone in the fire station knew that there would be work to do that day. They could feel it. The officers were all there, busy and excited—the chief, the commander, the brigade commander, and the head of the battalion. They formed work parties for firefighting, and for clearing roadblocks. One strong young firefighter clenched his fists. "Not the roadblocks, please," he thought to himself. He was fed up with doing other people's dirty work. Belgrade's firefighters are a division of the police, but he felt that this should not be made too much of. In any case they were used for everything and anything: driving police to Kosovo, washing the streets on the eve of celebrations because the municipal authorities couldn't rely on the city's sanitation department to do it, standing in at roadblocks when demonstrators had to be stopped.

"The Cacak firemen have lost their tanker," the base had been told that morning. "The police took it from them and put it on the road, then the protesters from Cacak arrived and smashed it up. It finished in a ditch!"

The young fireman heaved a sigh of relief. Four other men got into the unmarked black van without a word and headed for downtown. "Just stay cool," he thought. "All they have to do is sit tight, do nothing, and stay cool. They'll get through."

He had been assigned to one of three pump trucks, used to put out fires in buildings more than five stories high. The RTS building at 10 Takovska Street was five stories high.

While they waited for the heat of the day, the firemen got organized. They laid out old cables and set up makeshift aerials everywhere in the station so that they could hear the jammed signal of Radio Indeks. Then they turned on the television set in the Golden Nozzle, the club they had built for themselves above one of the truck stalls. The young fireman climbed on to the roof to adjust the antenna for TV Pancevo. Then they sat and waited. "Let's hope they don't issue us flak jackets and guns," moaned one of the men. From time to time they'd chip in to buy beer.

Below, in the mess room, three busloads of police officers who'd arrived from the towns of Leskovac, Vranje, and Pirot that morning were playing cards. "They used to send 20 buses," the fireman thought and looked back at the television screen. The convoys of protesters were just entering Belgrade.

The winner of the election, Vojislav Kostunica, left his apartment in Jevremova Street and set out for his party offices a few blocks away.

Vukasin Petrovic, one of the Otpor leaders, packed his backpack: vitamins, enough food for two days, files, a thousand and one sheets of paper, and two address books. He caught a cab.

Just along Knez Mihailova Street, across from the Otpor headquarters, was a restaurant called the Greek Queen. Petrovic went in and had a cup of coffee, then another. From there he went to one of Otpor's secure apartments, somewhere near the Zeleni Venac farmers' markets. He looked through the window. There were workmen setting up large microphones and video cameras on the building across the street. "State Security," he thought. "They're watching us, we're watching them."

Milan St. Protic expected a mêlée, so he wore riding boots and a belt with a broad buckle. He took his child to his grandmother instead of to kindergarten. By 10:30 he was with Patriarch Pavle. The elderly head of the Serbian Orthodox Church looked concerned. He, too, knew that it was now or never in Belgrade. When it began he telephoned Milosevic twice.

St. Protic asked for the Belgrade churches to ring their bells. He was promised something else: if anything dramatic happened, the patriarch would go out into the streets himself. Protic, the future mayor of Belgrade, left the Patriarchate in better spirits than when he had arrived. "He didn't ask for restraint," St. Protic said later. "Not a single word, not even a fatherly reproach for what we were planning to do."

It was ready to begin. But nobody yet knew how.

FOURTEEN

HIM OR US!

Police Headquarters, 29th November Street. Noon.

A field unit tells Avala 10: "Three thousand people heading for the Parliament from the Central Railway Station."

Avala 10: "Roger. Follow them."

Second field unit: "About 200 in Republic Square."

Third unit: "Here they come, from the direction of Belgrade Fairgrounds. They're on foot."

At 12:10 P.M., responds Avala 10: "Okay, follow behind them."

A unit in front of the Federal Parliament building cuts in: "They're coming! They're coming! They're moving toward the Parliament! The brigade has used tear gas!"

It still didn't look like a battleground. The domes of the Parliament were bathed in sunshine; the square, with its patches of lawn, concrete planters, and miniature fountains, was empty; traffic flowed normally through Nikola Pasic Square. Not a sign of police, despite the large numbers of Belgraders hurrying toward the Federal Parliament. The radio announced that the people from Cacak had arrived. The crowds flocked in from Terazije Square and Revolution Boulevard, from Kosovska and Vlajkoviceva Streets. They wanted to see what was happening. Buses and trucks were approaching, blowing their horns. The first bus appeared slowly from Kneza Milosa Street, turned toward the Parliament building, and pulled up on the street, right opposite the steps leading to the main entrance. A truck carrying a bull-dozer stopped behind it. Another bus impatiently mounted the sidewalk. The roadblock breakers climbed down from their buses and trucks. "These guys look mean. Very angry," recalls one Belgrade bystander, saying "This is going to get out of control."

Milder was the first one out of the bus in front of the Parliament. He was followed by the Zicer Café crowd, then the protesters from Cacak. These people weren't sightseers. They had come to Belgrade to do a job. Some of them ran straight for the steps up to the heavy, dark wooden doors of the Federal Parliament.

Nothing much happened at first. The police, about 30 of them, ran out of the Parliament building. The people from Cacak and Kraljevo withdrew and came to a halt about level with the Black Horses at Play, the giant pair of sculptures by the celebrated sculptor Toma Roksandic that guard either side of the broad steps up to the Parliament. The lines were drawn. One of the men from Cacak took a photograph.

Milder, Velja, Igor, and little Daca, Velja's bodyguards, scowling and cursing, faced the policemen, who were sweating under their flak jackets, batons, shields, and helmets. At the foot of the steps stood the angry men from Cacak, arms raised, fists clenched. For ten minutes or so they swore, spat, and slapped "He's finished" stickers onto the policemen's shields.

"What are you guarding?" Milder shouted.

"Who are you protecting?" roared Igor.

The first conflict started with an empty plastic bottle. Thrown from the crowd, it hit a policeman on the head. The clash lasted barely ten minutes. The police fired tear-gas canisters and drew their batons. Milder was in trouble. A canister landed at his feet as the policeman on the step above him swung his baton. Milder managed to protect his head, but the baton landed heavily on his hip. About a hundred demonstrators were literally swept off the steps.

"When you're surrounded by tear gas," Igor recalled, "you can't breathe and you can't see; your eyes are flooded with tears. What could we do? We ran. To Pioneer Park."

The square in front of the Parliament building was now deserted. Milder dragged himself, limping, back onto the bus. The wind carried the tear gas across Nikola Pasic Square. People were coughing even in Terazije, two blocks away. About a hundred yards farther, in Republic Square, Mladjan Dinkic, executive director of G17 Plus, completely carried away by the turn of events, was standing on a makeshift stage, chin up and one finger held high, shouting like a Russian Bolshevik revolutionary from 1917.

Publisher Predrag Markovic, another of the leaders of G17 Plus, was standing next to him with his arms crossed. Markovic isn't an easily excitable man. When someone in the crowd called his name he came down from the platform without hurrying.

It was a friend of Markovic's. "Tear gas! They've used tear gas . . . in front of the Parliament!" he said. He was gasping for breath.

Markovic put his hand on the man's shoulder. "Take it easy. We'll get going now." Then he asked Dinkic to stop his speech. After a muttered exchange with Markovic, Dinkic climbed back up to the stage. The revolution seemed about to begin.

"People!" Djindjic shouted. "The police in the Federal Parliament have just thrown tear gas at our friends from Cacak. Let's go there!" He pointed to the Parliament.

Police Headquarters, 12:22 P.M.

The unit in Republic Square alerted Avala 10: "They've just moved off from the square towards the Parliament building. The platform is also moving. It's on wheels."

Avala 10: "Roger."

Second unit: "The students have set out, too."

Third unit: "In front of the Politika building. They've reached Politika."

Avala 10: "Follow them. Follow them."

Checkpoint in Simanovci: "They've got through. They broke through. There are 50 buses on the way."

Avala 10: "Roger. Roger."

Checkpoint command at the National Hotel: "Ten buses passing."

Another unit: "New Belgrade Health Center. They're assembling."

Avala 10: "Roger. Roger. Follow them."

Another unit: "From Pozeska Street. Six thousand of them. With a bulldozer in front!"

It wasn't yet time for Vladan Batic, president of the Democratic Christian Party, to set out. At least not for the Yugoslav Parliament. Everything was ready at headquarters. "It's as though we're getting ready for the Battle of Kosovo," laughed Batic. People were arming themselves with whatever they could lay their hands on. Surrounded by his bodyguards, Batic set off for Simina Street. Belgrade was now in the streets. The Democratic Opposition of Serbia (DOS) leaders were scheduled to meet at noon.

Zarko Korac, the Social Democratic Union leader, was already on Simina Street, looking out the window. A woman was standing on the corner of Skadarljska and Simina Streets, dressed in her Sunday best, elegant, slim, smiling. Zarko would remember her all his life. Like a good omen.

He was interrupted by Misha Glenny, one of the foreign correspondents who knew the situation in the country well. "It's now or never, you know," said Glenny.

"I know that!" retorted Zarko, curtly.

There were no new decisions at the meeting, not even when a red-eyed Velja Ilic, co-president of the New Serbia, dressed in a dark blue sweatsuit, rushed into the room shouting, "They're shooting at us! They're completely insane!" There would be no backing down, said Democratic Party leader Zoran Djindjic. They drew up a list of speakers to address the mob after 3 P.M. The DOS leaders agreed to be in front of the Parliament at 5 P.M. Everything seemed to be going to plan.

"Time to go!" somebody called. Batic opened the door. He saw a pile of short lengths of metal pipe. The party secretary, Zika, was trying to conceal a bar under his jacket. When he left, at least seven inches of steel pipe was protruding from his jacket.

Batic went into the bathroom, took off his coat and shirt, and put a flak jacket on next to his bare skin. A mistake of the inexperienced: The bulletproof vest would pinch him the whole day.

In the meantime, Velja grabbed a sandwich. "We smashed them apart," he told a journalist, as he wolfed the food down.

A few yards away, Miroljub Labus, the chairman of the board of G17 Plus, took Djindjic by the hand. "Him or us!" he said.

"Him or us!" said Djindjic, squeezing his hand hard.

Police Headquarters. 12:57 P.M.

Avala 10 to a field unit: "Go to the Partizanski Road contractors' asphalt plant. Get road-building machinery and take it to Bubanj Potok. Block the road."

Field unit: "Roger."

Avala 10 to commanders of units from Vranje, Leskovac, and Pirot: "Half of you to Radio Television Serbia, half to the Parliament building! On the double!"

At 1:12 P.M., a field unit on Pancevo Bridge: "There's a bulldozer coming from Pancevo!"

Avala 10: "Follow it!"

Another field unit: "Milosa Pocerca Street. Dusanova Street. There's a truck here with a public address system. Kneza Milosa Street is blocked. Here come more! A hundred buses from Zrenjanin!"

Avala 10: "Roger, Roger."

G17 Plus leaders Dinkic and Markovic had already covered a lot of ground. They passed the Parliament building, now calm again. They walked down Kneza Milosa Street, through Nemanjina and Slobodana Penezica Krcuna Streets. They stopped at the Palace of Justice to file criminal complaints. Then back again, this time through Slavija Square and Srpskih Vladara Street. When they reached the Beogradjanka building they heard voices shouting: "Studio B! Studio B!"

"Let's go in," suggested Dinkic.

Markovic shrugged. "Why not!"

Nobody stopped them. They went straight to the twenty-second floor. Dinkic approached a security guard. "We want to see the director," he demanded.

"Only one of you," the security guard said.

That was all right by Markovic. He was dead tired in any case. He sat in an armchair outside the director's office. His cell phone rang. "Where are you?" asked Miroljub Labus.

"We're here at Studio B," Markovic began.

"Get out of there, for Christ's sake!"

"Why?"

"It's the one thing that's all tied up. We have a team inside. Get out of there fast!"

"So much for coordination," thought Markovic. He ran into the office. It wasn't easy getting Dinkic out. He was just taking over Studio B, or so he thought.

Police Headquarters. 1:43 P.M.

Field unit to Avala 10: "I'm at the asphalt compound of the Partizanski Road builders. We can't do anything. One machine is missing, and there's no key in the other one. The driver's not here. What shall I do?"

Avala 10: "Nothing . . . nothing. Never mind."

The opposition plan was falling apart. The convoys from Novi Sad, Sabac, and Srem hadn't reached Belgrade. Velja's attack on the Parliament had come too soon. The people in the buses had heard that the fighting had already begun, both at the Federal Parliament and on Branko's Bridge. Now nobody even dreamt of going to the airport or the federal government building in New Belgrade. Nothing could have been further from their minds. They parked outside the former Communist Party Central Committee building, a tall tower now broken and blackened with smoke. It had been one of the favorite targets of the NATO bombing campaign. From there they had to cross the river on foot into the city's center.

The convoys from Nis and south Serbia were late. Maki was standing on the square in front of the Belgrade University philosophy department. He was furious. The Otpor people wanted to march through the streets. He wanted to attack. Immediately.

Stanko Lazendic, the Otpor activist from Novi Sad, didn't hear him. He was among the crowd that had just arrived at the square. It looked pretty good to him. "He's finished!" Stanko kept repeating to himself. "He doesn't stand a chance," he shouted into his uncle's ear. The roars of the protesters from Novi Sad were still ringing in their ears. They were chanting "Novi Sad is coming, Novi Sad is coming, here's our town," as they hurried through the reverberating Belgrade streets on their way to the philosophy department.

Maki was rushing to the Parliament. "You just keep marching," he tells Otpor. "I'm off to do the job." His fury subsided along the way. "Fuck it!" he thought to himself. "Maybe they have a plan, too. Who cares!"

Stanko, Milan, and their uncle were rolling along with the marchers. There was no end to them. It took more than 20 minutes for the crowd to cross Republic Square as they headed toward Beogradjanka. It was there, in DOS's plan, that the critical mass of people should gather. In Terazije Square, some of the marchers became impatient. They turned toward the Federal Parliament.

Stanko wanted to get to Beogradjanka as per the plan. It was hopeless. The place was already jam-packed. There wasn't a square foot in the central area of Belgrade that wasn't crammed with people between 1 and 3 P.M. on October 5. "Let's head for the Parliament," he said to his uncle, and turned around. He took a bottle of water from his backpack and a pair of socks that he planned to wet. "To protect against the tear gas," he explained.

Radio Indeks reporter Jovan Palavestra saw the protesters wetting cotton balls, handkerchiefs, socks. "What are these people doing?" he asked himself. Palavestra knew about demonstrations—he had covered them for years, and he knew from experience that in a brawl between demonstrators and police, the police always win. It had always been that way. He saw no reason for it to be any different this time.

Palavestra didn't change his mind even when one vast mass of students encountered another on the corner of Kneza Milosa and Srpskih Vladara Streets. The second group was from Pozeska Street. "Oh my God! What the hell is this?" Palavestra asked in amazement when he saw the bulldozer with two tiny figures in the cab. "It must be revolutionary set-dressing," he thought. "It couldn't be meant as a weapon!"

The man in the bulldozer was grim-faced. "There are too many of us for them," Joe said to Milan the baker as he pointed at the mass of protesters blocking their way. "We'll fuck them anyway." He leaned on the horn.

Palavestra and the student marchers headed for the new destination, the Municipality of Vracar building, which, since the day before, had been the home of TV Vracar, the first free television station in Belgrade in six months. That march, too, proved to be unnecessary. There were plenty of men to guard TV Vracar. Well-armed men. The students wound through the narrow streets of the old district of Vracar to reach Revolution Boulevard. Once there, they rushed toward the Parliament. Palavestra still wasn't convinced. He had no faith in either the revolution or the bulldozer.

At the same time the DOS headquarters was relocating. From the Proleterskih Brigada Street offices of the Democratic Party, the DOS leaders moved to No. 3 Terazije Square. There they installed themselves behind the armored doors protecting the offices of Nebojsa Covic's Democratic Alternative. The narrow staircase next to the elevator, the only access to Covic's party headquarters, was packed with armed men. Inside were the DOS coordinators: Covic, Djindjic, Democratic Party leader Ceda Jovanovic, and the newly arrived Pedja Markovic, the delegate from G17 Plus. Djindjic's wife, Ruzica, stayed close to her husband. Covic had relocated his family. The children were with his parents-in-law in a guarded house in the town of Zeleznik. His wife was in their home on the slopes of Kosutnjak, with a dozen guards outside.

Just after 2 P.M. there was subdued panic at the headquarters. There had been no contact at all with Zoran Zivkovic, the leader of the protesters from the south. The convoy from the west had failed to surround the buildings assigned to it. At that time none of the DOS leaders knew exactly what was happening in the city. Djindjic looked ashen.

It turned out to be an advantage that the opposition army was so scattered, because there were so many people, far more than ever before. It's unlikely that the police could have dealt with such a large, dispersed crowd even if they had had many more than the three thousand confused officers in the city that day.

On October 5, something like a chain reaction happened in Belgrade.

Velja stopped the protest at the Parliament; Dinkic started out from Republic Square to arrive at the Palace of Justice; Stanko and the other protestors from Novi Sad swarmed onto the bridge and continued to the philosophy department. Then the people from Pozeska Street flooded into Kneza Milosa Street; there were huge masses of people in Revolution Boulevard, Nemanjina Street, and Vasina Street and blockades in Dorcol, New Belgrade, and Slavija. And from all sides, from all approaches to the city, the police units were shouting into their walkie-talkies: "Bulldozer! Bulldozer!"

It was simply not stoppable.

Slobodan Cerovic, the Serbian tourism minister and the president of the Yugoslav Left's Belgrade City Committee, watched the demonstrators from the Metropol hotel, about half a mile from the Parliament down Revolution Boulevard. "There are going to be more than half a million of them," he told his companions at the table.

Some of the demonstrators were with Goran Svilanovic, the leader of Civil Alliance of Serbia. The people from Uzice parked their vehicles near the Red Star soccer stadium. Billboards had appeared overnight, proclaiming "Belgrade: The Heart of Serbia."

The trumpeters were playing Chetnik evergreens like "From Topola to Ravna Gora." Svilanovic was smiling nonstop. The people of Belgrade, recognizing him, were astonished to see a prominent person like Svilanovic at the head of the marchers, screaming "Get ready Chetniks, there's battle ahead!"

Svilanovic led his group up and down the hills of Belgrade. From the Dedinje Street traffic interchange at Autokomanda to the National Library (where they danced to give the trumpeters a rest), down to Slavija Square, then up along Beogradska Street with another break for the trumpeters and another *kolo*, the traditional Serbian folk dance, then on to the law school.

Now they were just a few blocks away from the Parliament. Svilanovic hurried ahead to his party's new offices at No. 3 Terazije Square, a building accessible only from a narrow alley, along which are housed the headquarters of most of Serbia's opposition parties.

He protected himself against tear gas with a makeshift mask. It was simple: a cotton ball soaked in water, cling wrap over that, and a rubber band around his ears. Then he headed for Simina Street. There at the Gulliver Café, in front of the DOS headquarters, Velja Ilic and Milan St. Protic, the co-presidents of New Serbia, were sipping their espressos. "I'll have one too," said Svilanovic. A little later the three of them set out together for the Parliament.

Colonel Buha of the Belgrade Police Brigade was still waiting to be replaced at the strip mine in Kolubara. He'd been waiting since 9 A.M., when Avala 10 had told him: "Wait, wait. Something's happening here." Then at 2 P.M., Avala 10 again: "Leave one company there, only one! Bring the rest to Belgrade, fast!"

"Look after them for me," Colonel Buha told the miners, indicating his troops.

Bumping along the Ibar Highway in the jeep, he thought "Fuck it! Just when I thought I could take it easy!"

As he approached Belgrade Avala 10 called him again. "Where am I going?" he asked.

"To Dedinje!" (A neighborhood in Belgrade.)

"What the hell am I going to do in Dedinje?" the enraged Buha shouted. "And where the hell are my men?" When he heard they were on Ilije Garasanina Street his reply was curt: "Then that's where I'm going, too."

The roadblocks were ridiculous, he knew. How did the police think they could stop the opposition? By firing? He waved the thought away. "Nobody is going to fire."

"They wouldn't dare fire," said Marko Vukovic to the Delije, the group of Red Star fans assembled near the McDonald's in Terazije Square. "There are too many people. The cops won't dare shoot!" He had come on foot, all the way from Pasino Brdo, and had seen the city packed with people.

Ivan Nikolic, the restaurant worker, was sitting next to him, telling him about the heroes of the coal mine. He'd seen them on the Old Obrenovac Road, those grim men with sullen faces, heading in trucks and buses for Belgrade, their clenched fists raised. "You should see how many of them there are," Ivan said. And then he said: "So what if they do decide to fire. A few dead and . . . what then? Rebellion, brother! War! We'll stick it to them!" They set out towards the Parliament.

Zoran Timic was on the roof of one of the buses from Cacak. Tima, as he was known, was president of the Zvezdara Committee of the Democratic Christian Party of Serbia, a Red Star soccer fan by birth, always at the center of action of that wild tribe of fans, the Delije. Now he was knocking back a beer, waiting. His outward calm gave no indication that he had been waiting ten years for this. He looked over the vast square: "Where's my wife?"

She was there somewhere. She'd said she'd be there for as long as it took to get to the moment they'd been waiting for. "I'm going there today, and I'm not coming back until the job is finished," she had said. Tima knew his wife, and he knew when to believe her. "Today's the day," he thought and took another mouthful of beer.

"Son of a bitch!" swore Otpor leader Vukasin Petrovic. The computer they were using had just broken down. "Never mind," he decided, "I'll go home." He ran through the center of the city. "Great!" he thought. "Great! People everywhere!"

Police Headquarters. 2:37 P.M. Bubanj Potok field unit to Avala 10: "Eight buses coming from the direction of Nis. Hundreds of cars. They're here, at our barricade."

Avala 10: "Hold out."

Bubanj Potok field unit: "How? There are only 30 of us. Hey! They've gone straight through!"

Several units report in to Avala 10 at the same time: "Groups from Terazije on the move. Branko's Bridge. The bridge!"

Unit at Parliament, 2:40 P.M.: "Fifteen thousand people!"

Unit at Parliament, 2:47 P.M.: "Sixty-five thousand people!"

Unit at Parliament, 3:01 P.M.: "Seventy thousand!"

"Holy mother!" Radio Indeks reporter Jovan Palavestra's skepticism had just been dispelled. He was perched on a concrete planter near the Vuk

Karadzic monument, looking toward Parliament. The mob was flowing down the streets, waving flags and clenched fists.

An Air Force helicopter flew low over the center of Belgrade and the Parliament building. Apparently Army Chief of Staff Nebojsa Pavkovic was also keen to know how many people were there. Nobody believed the reports on the police radio.

Thousands of heads in front of the Parliament turned to the sky. Tima shook his fist from the bus, parked opposite the steps leading to the main entrance of the building. Milder heard only the growl of the chopper's engine. He was still lying across the seat in his bus, rubbing his hip, still hurting from the officer's baton. Maki took no notice. A young man climbed the flagpole in front of the Parliament and slapped a "He's finished" sticker across the police video camera transmitting the events live to the city police headquarters.

"I'm going to attack the Parliament!" Maki shouted to a policeman standing nearby. "Fuck off or I'll thrash the shit out of you!"

The policeman forced a grin.

"Hey!" roared Maki, "I've got armed men with me. Get out of the way!"

He pinched the policeman's cheek. Behind him, Maki's guys, wearing their backpacks, growled like bulldogs. "Motherfuckers."

The color drained from the policeman's cheeks. This was exactly what Maki had wanted. To look ferocious, to make them nervous.

He sent a few of his men around to the back of the Parliament. "When you hear a ruckus that means I've started. Then set it alight. First the cars, then the building."

Stanko, together with his brother and his uncle, installed himself at the monument to the Serbian commanders of World War I in Pioneer Park. Marko and Ivan were with the Delije at the edge of the park, opposite the main entrance to the Parliament.

Gigo, Bubac, and Sekula were standing by the flagpole at the bottom of the steps. "We're going in," thought Bubac. "That's for sure."

Sekula confronted a bald policeman who looked like an atheist to him: "Come on, cross yourself, for God's sake!"

An old woman asked a boyish policeman, "What are you doing here, sonny?"

A few yards away a man approached Zarko Korac.

"Hey!" he shouted, "It's seven past three! What are you waiting for?"

→← →← →←

3:08 P.M. Field unit at the Parliament to Avala 10: "Velja Ilic is making a speech!"

Peca threw his spoon down on the plate. "Fuck them!" he said. "Nothing's going to happen, again!" He didn't want to go today. People like him from the inner-city Dorcol area of Belgrade never missed an opportunity like this. Besides, who had fought the police on March 9, 1991?

"We did, the people of Dorcol!" Peca told his wife, Ivana. She was trying to find a radio station. On Dorcol's Jevrejska Street, the lowest-lying part of Belgrade, there was no clear signal to be found. "Shit!" Peca got up from the table. "God knows how many times and still nothing, fuck them!" "Shut up," his wife suddenly broke in. "I've got it. Radio Indeks! Something's happening . . ."

3:10 P.M. Avala 10 to a brigade commander near the Parliament: "Take half your men in. Straightaway!"

Colonel Buha reached Ilije Garasanina Street. His deputy, with the revolutionary name of Vladimir Ilic, was already there. "Who are our neighbors?" asked Buha, using military slang.

"I've no idea who's on either side," the deputy replied.

"Christ Almighty!" Buha was furious at the lack of communication: "What are we supposed to do?" he asked.

"No idea. Nobody knows anything," said Ilic.

"It's ready," said Vukasin Petrovic's mother when he returned home, as she whitewashed the wall. He grabbed his computer. Everything was clear to him. "She's taken some tranquilizers and started painting," he thought. She would be preoccupied that day. "It'll be okay," he told her as he ran out of the door.

3:15 P.M. Field unit at the Serbian Presidency to Avala 10: "Dinkic is here with some other people. He's asking to see President Milutinovic."

Avala 10: "Who cares!"

"The president isn't here," said a confused security guard. Behind G17 Plus Executive Director Mladjan Dinkic's back the whole of Pioneer Park and the square in front of the Parliament could be seen. Also thousands and thousands of flags and a mobile platform. "All right," said Dinkic, producing his business card. "Give him this." President Milutinovic would use the card later that same day, calling the G17 Plus office and asking, "Who can I talk to?"

Dinkic turned around. He couldn't move any further. The crowd was becoming agitated.

3:23 P.M. Field unit at the Parliament to Avala 10: "They've turned off our camera here. The demonstrators. The same one who put the sticker on it; he's climbed up again and turned it off!"

Christian Democratic Party President Vladan Batic was on the stage. Behind him, in front of the Parliament building, his party banner was fluttering in the breeze. The whole area seemed to be swelling. From the stage he could see everything, to the far side of Pioneer Park, to the left toward Kneza Milosa Street and Revolution Boulevard, to Takovska Street, the whole Parliament and, on the other side, Terazije and Nikola Pasic Squares.

"It's completely packed with people," Batic thought, as he read the letter to the demonstrators from Serbian Orthodox Archbishop Artemije of Kosovo. From somewhere close by he heard the screech of a bulldozer's horn. Batic raised his eyes from the paper. The crowd was growing larger by the minute.

3:27 P.M. Field unit at the Parliament to Avala 10: "A bulldozer in Kneza Milosa Street!"

"Fuck the bastards!" screamed Joe as the Parliament building rose into view. Milan the baker was urging him on: "Put your foot down! Step on it! Let's give it to them!"

Tima was now standing on the roof of the bus. Someone grabbed him by the shoulder: "These guys are full of shit," he said. "Come on, let's go!" They jumped down into the crowd.

Stanko's height gave him a view across the crowd. "It's started! It's started!" shouted the people standing on the kiosk at the corner of Nikola Pasic Square and Kneza Milosa Street. "Break through! Break through!" Marko ordered the Delije.

"The doors!" shouted Sekula, and he ran up the steps.

From one of the Cacak trucks, Goran Svilanovic could see flags waving.

Tima and his mates were already at the cordon. A policeman was giving a gas mask to a girl. "Out of the way!" Tima said to a policeman with a moustache and a large helmet.

"Move!" Maki shoved the policeman in front of him aside.

FIFTEEN

THE ASSAULT ON THE PARLIAMENT

The battle for the Parliament was over in exactly 37 minutes. When it began, at 3:32 P.M., Christian Democratic Party leader Vladan Batic was addressing the crowd from the mobile stage. The stage began to shudder. "This wasn't planned," thought Milan St. Protic, and he jumped from the shaking platform, convinced that the whole DOS plan had just shattered into as many pieces as there were people in front of the Parliament. "It's all going down the drain," he thought, watching the protesters running at the Parliament. "Calm down! Calm down!" he shouted. He threw his hands in the air.

The police from the Federal Police Brigade, with their reinforcements from Vranje, Leskovac, and Pirot, were helpless. There were too few of them. They managed to form a fairly strong double cordon at the foot of the Parliament steps and that was it. There was no cordon to the left or the right, in the gardens on Vlajkoviceva Street or those in Takovska Street around the ends of the two wings of the building. There was nothing to stop the crowd at any of the usual police control points.

From the side of the steps the police were fanned out around the arc formed by the demonstrators: close to the steps there was one every couple of feet; from the corners of the building they thinned out, first to one every three feet, then one every six feet, nine feet, twelve; at the edges of this swelling mass of humanity there were no police at all. DOS security guards were keeping the peace, but they weren't inclined to be hard on the burgeoning crowd.

"The hand of God was guiding them," Sekula of Kraljevo said later. It's easy to see why he thought so. At about 3 P.M. the crowd stretched sideways to the edges of the parks flanking the imposing Parliament building. The lack of police and the constant inward flow of people had an effect. By 3:30 the front row had moved some 50 yards toward the Parliament stairs.

The long flight of stairs is broken by a broad landing about a third of the way up, reached from both sides by paved vehicle access ramps. At about 3:20 P.M. a child no more than two years old ran up the ramp from Vlajkoviceva Street as cameras clicked. The same ramp was used a couple of minutes later by a young man in a red sweat suit. Waving a banner, he reached the upper flight of steps. A policeman grabbed him by the arm.

Other demonstrators were already coming from the opposite side of the Parliament building. They needed to cover only a hundred yards or so to be in behind the double police cordon at the bottom of the steps. The police no longer had a chance.

Maki was at the very center. "Off I go!" he said to himself and moved the policeman facing him aside. He neither punched nor pushed him, just brushed him aside with one hand and went on. He ran up the steps. Someone to the left of him fell, carrying a banner. Maki tried to seize the banner.

"Let it go, fuck you," shouted the young guy, wrapping his legs around the flagstaff and hanging on for dear life.

"He thinks I'm a policeman," thought Maki. He headed for the door. There were angry people running to the right and left of him. The police, facing the crowd, backed up the steps of the Parliament. Some clung to the flanks of the giant horse sculptures. At the upper landing, other police hugged the stone guardhouses on either side of the door.

Tima wasn't interested in beating them. There was no need for that. He made his way through the police cordon and ran up the steps, taking them three or four at a time, waving his arms to the others to join him as he approached the main doors.

"Come on! Let's go!" The police at the top were petrified.

"Take their helmets! Take their helmets! Take everything!" he shouted. There wasn't a word of protest. The riot gear was falling by itself while the police stood in shock. People were taking whatever they wanted from them.

Gigo and Sekula kept looking back. Bubac had been behind them a moment before.

"Fuck it!" Sekula said. There were already people at the door. He ducked a burly policeman, the only one still attempting to defend himself, swinging his baton every which way. "To the doors!" he yelled. "To the doors!"

Gigo followed without a moment's thought. He had counted on there being thousands of police inside the building. The first wave at the door would be the first to die, he reckoned. Throwing his life to the winds, he raced up the stairs.

Bubac was right behind, but he couldn't see them. All he could see was the big policemen swinging his baton into anyone who came his way. The concrete planters by the steps were already smashed. Bubac didn't think much. "I have to say," he said later, "I didn't know the man; I'm sorry, but I aimed at his head. And I wanted to. Fuck it!" The policeman raised his shield and one leg, just for an instant. The rock broke his leg. Bubac saw the man fall. The crowd was already stampeding over him. "The kids will kill him!" thought Bubac. Then he smelled tear gas.

At 3:33 P.M. police command station Avala 10 asked for more police troops to be brought to the Parliament building.

"Chemicals!" came the order from police headquarters. "Use chemicals!"

In 1974, Yugoslavia signed a particularly vague UN document banning toxins, any chemical substance which, when used for a particular purpose or in a particular way, resulted in physiological malfunction of human, animal, or plant organisms. By this definition, toxic gases were used in Belgrade on October 5. These gases were the kind used for temporary incapacitation. Some of these gases are CS, CR, and CN, types of tear gas. CS was used that day at the Parliament, at the Radio Television Serbia (RTS) building, and near the police station in Stari Grad. It is the strongest of the poisonous gases above, which means that a very low concentration is enough to achieve the desired effect. CS is known as "police toxic gas."

Colonel Dragan Joksimovic, the head of the Poison Control Center of the Military Medical Academy in Belgrade, was in the square in front of the Parliament that day by pure chance. He recognized the characteristic smell of CS. "Tear gas," he thought, "nothing serious." Sneezing and tear gases are lethal only if, for instance, they are directly injected into a vein, forming cyanides. However, they are also dangerous if used in large quantities in a closed area. The Parliament building looked like one large, sealed space.

Maki had to be the first there, too. He stood with his shoulders against the door. "One! Two! Push!" the people around him shouted. The door creaked and gave way. "Literally at the second attempt!" Maki was surprised. Both of the doors opened together.

The revolutionary from Valjevo hesitated. A man in civilian clothes was sitting at a desk to the right of the lobby. "A civilian!" Maki was astonished. For a moment they looked at each other, wide-eyed. Then the man jumped up, swinging open the lid of a cardboard box he held in his hands. He threw the box toward the door. Maki barely saw the man putting on a mask and fleeing somewhere inside the building. Smoke was pouring from the box. Right into his face. This was the first tear gas used against the demonstrators that afternoon as they rushed the Parliament.

CS gas works on the nerve endings, stinging the nose, eyes, and lungs with an increased flow of tears and saliva. There is also an increase of secretion in the lungs, causing coughing and vomiting.

These things all happened to Maki at once. He couldn't breathe. His eyes were watering. He thought he was going to throw up, right there in the doorway. "Step back! Back!" he told himself. At least his mind was still clear. He tried to turn around. The crowd, surging through the broken door, was propelling him forward. Straight toward the police pouring out of the vast Parliament chamber into the lobby, masks on their faces and tear-gas guns in their hands. "A rain of tear gas," Maki described it later, "that's what it was."

The police pointed their tear-gas guns at the high ceiling of the lobby. They were standing less than ten yards from the demonstrators. Had they aimed at the crush of people there would have been casualties. The tear-gas cartridges ricocheted off the stucco ceiling and fell, smoking, on the heads of the crowd. People crushed into the doorway from both sides: some to get in, others to get out. They crashed into one another and fell. Maki dragged himself away, leaning against the wall. His strong, fit legs and sheer good luck somehow helped him to get out.

Once outside, still blinded, he began to take equipment from the police in the cordon, leaning hard against the stone booth beside the doors. He stripped the gear from the police as though they were dolls. "Give it to me! Let it go!" He was coughing and throwing various bits of gear behind his back. Masks, shields, batons. He kept a mask, a helmet, a walkie-talkie, and a pistol for himself. A huge crowd of choking demonstrators rushed out of the Parliament lobby in a crowd of acrid smoke. Smoking cartridges were flying over their heads. Maki was swept away, falling down again and again before reaching the bottom of the steps.

Sekula was running up the steps. "The doors!" he shouted. "Come on!" He turned around to see that rolling ocean of humanity once more. "We'll make it!" he thought. Then, looking back at the entrance, he had to concede defeat. From the top of the stairs, from the doorway, people were falling, tumbling over one another, all the way to his feet. There was smoke pouring out, and tear-gas cartridges whizzing past. He ended on the broad pavement at the foot of the stairs. More people were still running in from Takovska Street, with no idea what was going on.

Marko and Ivan were running toward the Parliament from Pioneer Park, Marko in front, Ivan right behind him. A tear-gas cartridge hit the man next to Ivan in the head. The man didn't let out a cry, just fell to the ground next to him. Ivan himself was already vomiting. The smoke from the cartridge had gone straight down his throat. Marko continued on through the door. A few yards inside he, too, began to throw up. He had run straight into the densest cloud of smoke. "Get out of here!" he told himself.

Five Otpor guys formed a wedge, Stanko Lazendic at the peak. "Move away! Get away!" they shouted, trying to hold the crowd back. It took them less than a minute. They vaulted the planters and ran up the ramp but were forced back by tear gas. Stanko was holding dampened socks over his mouth and nose. He couldn't breathe. The stampede carried him across the road to the small park next to the post office.

Goran Svilanovic jumped down from the truck. His wife's words were ringing in his head. "Go and finish the job! Go and finish the job!" she had said. He pushed at the people in front of him shouting "Come on! Let's go!" The tear gas caught him about ten yards from the steps. He tried to protect himself with his improvised mask but he was still choking. He threw the mask away and walked down the side of the huge building. There had to be another way in.

Tima just stood there. And Gigo. There were people running toward them and people running the other way. The ones in front were bumping into one another and falling down. The barrels of the tear-gas guns protruded through the doors. Someone shouted, "Come on, fuck it! They can't kill us all. Let's go!" A few yards away, Bubac ran up against a wall of people and teargas. "Fucking bastards!" he said and turned to run toward Pioneer Park.

"They're running away!" said Ivana. That was all she could hear through the static on the radio. "Who is?" shouted Peca. "Not now! Where are they running to now?" Ivana shrugged. "Probably . . ." she began and then realized she was alone. Peca was already in the street. "There's no backing out now!" he was shouting as he ran. "No backing out!"

"They've beaten us!" thought Otpor's Vukasin Petrovic, as he reached Republic Square. The crowd was still running from the Parliament. Only one thought was on his mind as he entered Otpor's safe apartment: to lock the door behind him.

SIXTEEN

PARLIAMENT FALLS

3.39 P.M. Field units at Parliament to Avala 10: "They're throwing things! They're coming back! They're coming back! There are more of them."

Avala 10: "Follow those groups. Follow wherever they go!"

Field commander at Parliament to Avala 10: "I've used the chemicals. No effect!"

Field unit at Parliament: "They've broken a lot of windows. They're militant. Very militant!"

Another officer, arriving at the Parliament as reinforcement, calls Avala 10: "I've entered the building! I hear they're going to attack from Kosovska Street. There are people injured here! Send backup!"

Avala 10: "Organize defense from the inside!"

Officer inside Parliament: "There are windows being smashed on all sides. There's a lot of smoke here. I can hardly see anything! Now they've broken the windows facing Kosovska Street!"

Avala 10: "Watch the situation. Don't let them get close! You know what you have to do."

Officer: "There aren't enough men here. They can easily get in from Kosovska Street!"

The Social Democratic Union leader Zarko Korac was clinging to the right flank of the Parliament building as he dragged himself toward Kosovska Street. He'd already taken a lot of tear gas, and he'd seen people falling down the steps from the main entrance. "They'll shoot!" he thought. "They're going to shoot!" He clung even more tightly to the wall but moved away when the windows above his head began to break.

In Kosovska Street people were already pushing garbage containers around. There were stones flying at the police cars parked there. The demonstrators caught up with a policeman in full riot gear. A handful of guys were punching him only a few yards away from the entrance. Someone ran up and kicked him. "Don't do that!" somebody else shouted.

The faces of the people in Kosovska Street were twisted with anger. Two women turned away, unable to watch.

Another policeman, in everyday uniform, drew his gun from its holster. He pointed it at the people, then stopped and returned it to the holster. They chased him all the way to the back door of the Parliament. Then they started smashing up the cars.

Zarko watched in astonishment. How easy it looked! Five or six guys turned a Black Maria over in seconds. Then it burst into flames.

3.45 P.M. A field officer inside the Parliament to Avala 10: "There are a lot of them. They're smashing up the police cars!"

Avala 10: "As soon as you have a chance, take action!"

Officer: "They're surrounding us from the side, from the park. They're throwing everything they can get their hands on."

To Maki it all looked like a film by Sergei Eisenstein, the famous Soviet director whose films such as *The Battleship Potemkin* captured the chaos and emotions of demonstrations and rebellion. Crazy people flying down the stairs. He himself had fallen on the pavement and couldn't get up. His mouth and nose were full of vomit. He had lost the mask and the helmet, but the pistol and the walkie-talkie were still there. One of his men helped him back to his feet and dragged him toward the pine trees in the park near Takovska Street. About a dozen of the other guys were also gathered there. Maki regained his composure. "Set it on fire, fuck them, set it on fire!" The guys with the backpacks ran off.

3:48 P.M. Avala 10 to Avala 45: "Avala 45, start moving toward the building and take the equipment with you. Take action as soon as possible, beginning from the corner of Takovska Street."

"Understood," Belgrade Police Brigade Colonel Buha said, and glanced at his deputy, Ilic. "Our people in the Parliament building are calling for help," he said. "Whatever you say," Ilic replied curtly.

"Let's go!" said Buha. He ran out with 150 policemen following. As soon as they reached Takovska Street, Buha realized there were at least ten times as many demonstrators as had been reported on the police band. He couldn't have seen them before because the buildings lining Ilije Garasanina Street had blocked his view. They were behind him in Takovska Street, in front of him in Kneza Milosa Street, and at the side near the church of St. Marko. And there weren't a handful, not a hundred of them: there were thousands of demonstrators rushing toward him. "They're going to cut us off," he realized.

His men were firing tear gas. Avala 10 was shouting, "Hurry up! Take action as you go!"

Some of Buha's men stormed the Parliament building. A tear-gas cartridge, coming out of nowhere, landed at his feet. Buha didn't have a mask. He stopped, choking. Through the smoke in Kosovska Street he saw his men rushing from Parliament into the street. He ran into the entrance of a building at No. 43 Kosovska Street.

3:57 P.M. Avala 10 to unidentified unit: "Deploy forces and proceed to the back entrance."

Officer: "The commander of the Federal Brigade isn't here. I've redeployed the troops. I don't have enough men."

Avala 10: "Regroup. Don't let anyone get in!"

Milder managed to stand up in the aisle of the bus. Smoke was pouring out of the Parliament building. A man was throwing up beside the bus. "Open the door," Milder told the driver. "Relax," said the driver. "Lie down . . ." He didn't finish. Milder looked deadly serious. "Open up!" Milder repeated and tied a sweatshirt on his head, the Otpor clenched-fist logo covering his nose and mouth. He limped toward the Parliament. There was smoke gushing out of the main entrance. It looked impossible to get through. "I'm going to the right. I'll try to get in from the post office side," he told himself.

Sekula stood up. The wind was blowing toward the west, in the direction of the park on Vlajkoviceva Street. He shook his head and set off eastward. At the corner of the east wing of the Parliament he saw a man climbing up the building. "That's the way!" he thought and began climbing himself. He reached a small balcony on the first floor. The glass door was already broken. The man inside was throwing papers out through it.

"Fuck you!" swore Otpor's Stanko Lazendic. "You haven't come all this way to run away now. Get back!" People were crawling around him. A cartridge landed at his feet. He kicked it and walked off. The cartridge fell in front of a door. "Side entrance. Let's go!" he shouted. People began climbing down from the window above the door. "When did they manage to get in?" Stanko was amazed. The crowd rushed to the door. "Here folks!" shouted

Stanko, "Here's the entrance!" Images of ancient days sprang into his mind. Savage Avars assaulting a great Roman fortress. One man, stripped to the waist, was banging on the door. Stanko ran off toward Kosovska Street. He had lost his brother somewhere and had to find him.

The bulldozer approached the windows on the east wing of the Parliament. Steel grilles were snapping like toothpicks under the heavy scoop. "Come on, guys," shouted Joe. Milan the 72-year-old baker, fists clenched, was shouting, "Smash it, fuck them! Smash it!" There were Molotov cocktails hurled toward Parliament. The curtains were alight. "Lift us up, Chief," the men around the bulldozer shouted. Some of them ran into the scoop. Joe hoisted them up to the first floor. The rest swarmed up the bulldozer like ants. The first floor of the building was ablaze.

"Where do you think you're going, Bubac?" he asked himself. "Get back there!" He was weeping from the tear gas. "Don't chicken out!" he kept telling himself. He was soon on his way back in. He saw a priest on the stairs leading up to the main entrance. He was standing in his black robes, red-eyed, arms outstretched toward the square. As Bubac pressed ahead he heard the priest say: "Onward, brothers! Forward, heroes! Smash the Red Gang!"

"We will," thought Bubac. "You can count on it!"

Goran Svilanovic, a leader of Civil Alliance of Serbia, was climbing up the wall of the west wing. He had to get inside. He clutched at a window frame and peered into the room. There was already one protester inside, pushing furniture against the door. "Good for him," thought Svilanovic. "If they come in they'll cut him to pieces." In any case, that route was blocked. He jumped down and set off again for the main entrance.

Tima had been standing on the stairs the whole time. "Come on!" he was shouting. "Come on!" The crowd surged to and fro around him. It seemed that they wouldn't make it. Then someone hurled a bottle. And another. The entrance of the Parliament building burst into flames. "We've done it!" he thought.

4:00 P.M. Field officer at Parliament to Avala 10: "Access from Kosovska Street dangerously unprotected. One commander with head injuries from a rock."

Avala 10: "Take action!"

Officer: "They've got into the building from Takovska Street. They're demanding negotiations."

Avala 10: "Take action! Take action!"

Officer: "There's smoke in here: something may be burning. It's complete chaos."

Svilanovic managed to get into the building on his third try. There were about 30 policemen standing by a glass door in front of the main chamber. Svilanovic walked up to them. They looked nervous. He produced his identification.

"Good afternoon. I'm . . ."

"We know who you are, Mr. Svilanovic," said a police lieutenant. "Just stop them and everything will be all right."

The crowd was surging behind him.

"I can't stop them," said Svilanovic. "Is there an exit you can use to get out of here?"

"Stop them," the lieutenant repeated, "and everything will be all right. Stop them."

People were already running up to the police. "Give us the masks," they shouted. "Give us the masks!"

"Hang onto them," pleaded the lieutenant.

Svilanovic led the whole group toward the great hall. The Chamber of the Republics. The police took their helmets off. They'd had enough. One young policeman began to vomit. "He needs to get outside," said Svilanovic. He took the young officer by the arm and led him out of the hall. The furious mob ran toward them.

Sekula charged into the room. "They'll kill me if they get in here," he thought. The entire room was wood-paneled. Period chairs, tables, cabinets: he had to drag them all away from the door. "What if they kill me," Sekula thought again, "so what!" He pulled the furniture away roughly and burst into the corridor. He set about moving tables, chairs, cabinets, sofas. He finally burst out into the corridor. Windows were breaking left and right, people pouring in. He ran into the chamber.

He immediately recognized Svilanovic, who was leading a bare-headed policeman by the arm. The policeman looked pretty bad. The men rushing toward them looked even worse. "Beat the fuck out of them!" they were screaming.

"Why?" protested Sekula. "The police are Serbs too, and so is Svilanovic." He ran to help them. The policeman was choking. All three were showered with blows. "Man did they attack us!" Sekula said later. "They beat us for twenty minutes. They just kept hitting. We'd put our hands up, they'd punch us. We'd put them down again and they'd hit us in the head. We'd try to break between them and they'd thrash us again. They were punching the kid in the ribs, and he was shouting, 'They're going to kill me!' Then they'd punch us again. We barely managed to escape and get out near the little fountains. Then Svilanovic went down, and I lost track of him."

Sekula somehow dragged the policeman to Kosovska Street and into an apartment. An old woman gave him some water.

Peca, the protestor from New Belgrade, ran out into Republic Square. There wasn't a soul there. Barely 500 yards from the Federal Parliament building, Belgrade looked like a ghost town. He ran up Decanska Street. Milan St. Protic was rushing from the direction of Parliament. "I'm coming back!" he shouted to people who stopped him on the way. "I'm coming back. I have to get to the DOS headquarters!" Peca headed on toward the Parliament. At the popular Presernova Kleta Café, near the premises of the daily *Borba*, people were tearing up tablecloths. Peca recognized them—Tomica Matkovic and his crowd from primary school. He hadn't seen them for at least 20 years. He joined them, and they rushed on together.

The smoke hung thickly over the square. Coughing, Peca and the others made their way to the steps of Parliament. The man next to Peca was hit by a tear-gas cartridge as they reached the entrance. Peca clutched his throat. "I have to get out," he thought, and turned around. He didn't manage to take a single step. A man behind him demanded: "What do you think you're doing? Where are you going?"

"What's it to you?" choked Peca. "Get out of my way!"

The man was obstinate: "It's now or never," he said. "Turn around!"

Just for a moment, Peca thought about hitting him. Then his eyes cleared a little. They were eye-to-eye, but the man was standing at least three steps below. "Christ," thought Peca, "I'm not going to take this one on!" Around he turned to face the entrance. The crowd literally carried him inside. Sideways.

The first floor on the post office side was already ablaze. Milder, stripped to the waist, his Otpor sweatshirt over his face, was banging on the side door. His heart was racing when the door gave way. "Who's inside?" he asked himself. "Whoever it is, they're going to fire!" He went in. The corridors in the basement of the Parliament were oval in profile. The people traveling them were cautious and frightened, peering into room after room. One room was full of papers.

Milder struck a light. There was a hose lying in the corridor outside the room. They drank from it. "That's enough," said Milder. "That's our weapon!" Cautiously, pausing from time to time, they dragged the hose along the corridor. Suddenly tear gas poured around the curve of the narrow corridor.

"Ten of them!" shouted the guy in the lead.

Milder turned up the pressure on the hose and aimed the water jet at the police, while the rooms on either side burned. The police, in gas masks and drenched to the skin, were firing tear gas and sliding back, falling from the force of the water, getting up again. Then Milder threw the hose down and the crowd charged the policemen.

Milder grabbed for the nearest uniform, catching hold of a gas mask, while the policeman gripped the leather thong around Milder's neck. Both of them were straining. "Who'll give in first?" thought Milder. "He's going to strangle me!" He was already dizzy when he managed to pull the mask off. "Okay, you win!" the policeman said and let him go. Milder, still stripped to the waist and carrying a shield and a nightstick as trophies, ran up the steps to the main hall of the Parliament. He saw policemen being herded into the Chamber of the Republics. He hesitated: Did he want revenge? "I'm not an executioner," he finally thought, and he ran from the building.

Svilanovic managed to get to his feet. His watch was missing. "My father's watch!" He hurried back inside. The Parliament was ablaze. The tear gas was no longer choking him, but the smoke from the fire caught his lungs. He ran out again.

4:09 P.M. An officer in the Parliament to Avala 10: "A new wave of them from Majke Jevrosime and Vlajkoviceva Streets."

Another officer to Avala 10: "I've used all the chemicals. I don't have enough men."

Third officer to Avala 10: "The Parliament building has been taken."

Marko and Ivan were together again in the Parliament building. There were still police inside, frightened men with their hands in the air, left to the mercy of the mob swarming in. Marko and Ivan no longer wanted to attack them. "We only fight them when they're strong." Marko said later. "Otherwise it would have been pointless."

Milan Lazendic, the brother of the "domestic traitor," walked into the Parliament building through the main entrance with three other men. They found three disoriented policemen a foot and a half from the door, asking how to get out. "I want to go home," one of the policemen said.

"I've had enough." Milan and the others took the policemen's gas masks and walked on.

Inside, people were looting the building. One man was dragging an armchair bigger than himself. Milan went down to the basement. People were grabbing whatever they could lay their hands on from the restaurant: cartons of cooking oil, bottles, chairs, meat from the freezer. Milan snatched a bottle of vodka and one of strong Manastirka slivovitz, or plum brandy, and put them under his jacket. He walked out through the back door, into Kosovska Street.

Peca saw people snatching anything they came across. He wasn't sure how he felt about it. "I should get myself a trophy before they come back and tear us apart," he thought. He grabbed an armchair with one hand, then let go to reach for a stack of files containing biographies of the members of Parliament. Somebody had thrown them into the hall. When he turned around, the armchair was gone. He stuffed the files under his jacket.

Outside the Parliament building, President of Social Democracy Vuk Obradovic was standing on a ladder addressing the crowd. Smoke was still gushing from the entrance. Next to it stood St. Protic. "Go on in, Milan!" people were shouting, but he declined. "That's my place over there," he told them, pointing across Pioneer Park to the Belgrade City Assembly. The other DOS leaders were beginning to assemble.

4:17 P.M. Avala 10 to officers in the Parliament: "Deploy your units!"

There was no response.

SEVENTEEN

THE BATTLE OF VLAJKOVICEVA STREET

The war raged on. Police from several Belgrade police stations—Vozdovac, Zvezdara, Savski Venac, Vracar, and Stari Grad—were still trying to force their way through to the Parliament. Meanwhile, other police were attempting to flee from the back of the building, down the hill from Kosovska toward 29th November and George Washington Streets. In the area bordered by Takovska and Decanska Streets, fleeing policemen repeatedly ran straight into the hands of the demonstrators: they fought, tried to escape, hid, were found again, and finally surrendered. The centrally located Stari Grad police station was firing salvoes of tear gas the whole time. The streets were lined with burning cars and garbage containers.

The whole city, in one way or another, was involved. This was not the usual Belgrade scenario, with one of the main squares packed with thousands of demonstrators convinced that the government would topple at any minute while, a hundred yards down the road, thousands of shoppers bought carrots at the city's largest market, convinced the only thing likely to change in the country would be the prices. October 5 was different.

Those who weren't on the streets were listening to the radio; the lucky ones who could pick up TV Pancevo's signals were watching the scene relayed live from broadcast trucks parked in front of the Federal Parliament. Only the Serbian and Yugoslavian governments displayed no interest. The cabinets of Serbian Prime Minister Mirko Marjanovic and Federal Prime Minister Momir Bulatovic didn't meet that day. They were never to meet again. Slobodan Cerovic, the tourism minister in the Serbian government, giving his account for this book, said that no one from the government called him to any kind of meeting that day. "I don't know why," he said.

On October 5, some of the most important apparatuses of its power were being dismantled, and the regime was in disarray. Like other dictators before him, Slobodan Milosevic was paying dearly for his dislike of people who used their own heads and for his preference for sycophants and functionaries. When clear thinking and decisive action were essential, neither Serbian Prime Minister Marjanovic nor Federal Prime Minister Bulatovic knew what to think, let alone what to do. Milosevic cut them out of the game and turned to Police Minister Vlajko Stojiljkovic, who was unaware that the police were no longer obeying his orders, to Rade Markovic, head of the State Security Service, who was either uninformed or too well informed to allow himself to become more deeply involved, and to Nebojsa Pavkovic, chief of staff of the Yugoslavian Army, who didn't want to get involved at all.

What records exist suggest that Milosevic, through Police Minister Stojiljkovic, demanded special army troops to help guard the Parliament building. Fifteen men were promised, and police headquarters even informed the commander of the Federal Police Brigade to expect fifteen members of these special units.

There is no evidence that these men ever reached the Parliament building. They probably didn't, because the army's special units, no matter what they are securing, know only one way to do it, and that is by shooting. And not a single shot was fired from the Parliament building while the demonstrators were attacking it.

Furthermore, there was no one to command the federal police units during the assault because their commander had been the first to flee. Milosevic's principle of relying on obedient officials, which had spread like cancer through every vein of the system, backfired in this particular case on the unfortunate police officers, a unit unprepared for anything like October 5. They had been brought to the Parliament building from the guardhouses in front of various foreign embassies which it was their job to secure. They were loaded up with gear and forced to put their heads in the lion's mouth. Because of this, many people suspect that these 150 men had been sent deliberately and calculatingly. The theory goes that the regime had wanted the loss of police lives to galvanize the army into action and thus prevent its own downfall. However likely this theory may appear, a telephone conversation between Milosevic and Army Chief of Staff Pavkovic, recorded on the afternoon of October 5, gives the lie to it.

"The symbol of the state has been set on fire," said Milosevic.

"That's right," replied Pavkovic. "It has been set on fire, but it's empty. There have been no casualties. Nothing."

The idea of using the army to defend the symbols of the state came to Milosevic only once thousands of angry people had swarmed on the Parliament. It was a classic move of desperation. He had earlier attempted to fend off his downfall with bullets and hand grenades, miles away from Belgrade. Today, when at least part of the truth has surfaced, that move seems no less desperate. The outcome was inevitable. And once it had reached the capital, embittered and resolute, it was all over for the regime. Milosevic fell apart. And then he cried for help.

There are no police records that can establish why the other units failed to come to the assistance of their colleagues in the Parliament or Radio Television Serbia (RTS). Did they simply decide to disobey orders, or were they unable to comply? From the outside it looked as though the Belgrade police tried to do what they could without getting their hands too dirty. A lot of them were just not interested. Milan St. Protic recalls meeting a policeman on Vlajkoviceva Street the morning of October 6, in uniform and heading for work—to the Stari Grad police station, which had been ransacked and burned down the day before! "Do you know where you're going?" asked St. Protic. "Why?" the policeman replied. He had no idea what had happened in Belgrade the day before.

In early October he and his fellow police officers had been more concerned with saving their own necks than Milosevic's. While they were running around and fighting the crowds on the slopes near Kosovska Street during the assault on the Parliament, their one thought was how to escape alive.

There were moments of tragedy and others of pure comedy. In the end, all revolutions are alike.

October 5, 4:22 P.M. Avala 10 to unidentified officer: "Try to hold out, try to hold out. Help is on the way."

Radio Indeks reporter Jovan Palavestra was outside the Yugoslav Airlines office on Revolution Boulevard when the commotion began. He ran to the Parliament, a block away, stopping at the junction of Kneza Milosa and Takovska Streets. "It's like a comic strip," he thought. Crowds of demonstrators armed with clubs were running toward the Parliament. The monumental edifice was already ablaze on one side. Clouds of black smoke were pouring from the back of the building. Tiny puffs of smoke were coming from the main entrance across the small square in front. Palavestra ran up Kosovska Street. At the corner of Palmoticeva Street, two cars were on fire. That would explain the black smoke.

Two women were trying to get into the post office building on the corner of Palmoticeva and Kosovska Streets. They were choking, banging on the door. The staff inside, visible through a narrow window, waved them off. "No way! No way!"

Palavestra put in a live report to Radio Indeks. The rules of journalism had gone out the window. "I hope somebody smashes the windows of the post office!" he shouted. Radio Indeks had become an active participant in the revolution.

He was cut short by a stampede. People were running hysterically from the square, straight into Palmoticeva Street. Police had appeared out of nowhere, sweeping their batons in front of them and apparently firing tear gas. Palavestra dived into an apartment building on the corner, across the road from the post office (some kindly residents took him in). There, from a first floor window, he watched the show. First the police stood on the corner, firing tear-gas cartridges, then chased the demonstrators down Palmoticeva Street. Then they returned. Only this time the demonstrators were chasing the police.

4:30 P.M. Avala 10 to field officer: "Use chemicals! Now!"

Officer to Avala 10: "I'm using them, but they're not reacting. They're not reacting to the tear gas!"

Ceda Jovanovic was making a speech. Something about beatings, about the number of demonstrators and the number of police. Swearing at them! This was all happening in Decanska Street, near the Youth Cultural Center. There he stood, defying anyone to back off. "Only forward," he cried. "Only straight ahead!"

New York Times foreign correspondent Stephen Erlanger was amazed. He had seen Ceda just a few minutes earlier rushing from Nebojsa Covic's Democratic Alternative Party office with a dozen other people. It had been pure, unadulterated revolutionary wrath. Ceda was ready to kill and be killed. In either case, he was determined to win. He was still in this mood in Decanska Street as he blocked the way back. "If we don't get the better of him [Milosevic] today, he'll have the better of us as long as we live!" Ceda was shouting. Nearly five hundred people stormed off behind him down Kosovska Street.

Ceda first saw the police on the corner of Kondina Street. "Pigs!" he and the others yelled, over and over, a war cry. The police looked like devils to Ceda, with their shields and masks, batons drawn. But he and his men looked even worse to the men in uniform. A howling mob with sticks, rocks, crowbars, and other assorted weapons in their hands and on their belts, screaming and roaring down Kosovska Street. The police turned pale.

"It just erupted," Ceda said later. Five hundred people at full tilt into forty-odd police. "It blew up! Boom!" Ceda later found a rubber bullet stuck between his vest and his flak jacket.

The police dispersed, some to Kondina Street, others to Kosovska Street. The ones left behind were simply trampled by the mob. They were stripped of their gear: guns, helmets, masks, and shields. The crowd caught the rest on the next corner, outside a small tailor's shop.

The police clung desperately to the shop window. "We surrender! We surrender!" they shouted. The mob ground into them, punching, kicking, battering them with crowbars. Ceda jumped onto the hood of a car, clearly hearing it crunch beneath his weight. "Stop it!" he shouted, holding his hands up. His men pulled the enraged horde away from the police. "Stop it!" waved Ceda. "They've surrendered! They're finished!" He turned to the battered, disheveled policemen. "Fuck you and your Milosevic!" he yelled at them. "Is he fucking worth it? Go home, the lot of you."

The police vanished. He didn't even see which way they went. He was busy throwing up. It hadn't hit him until it was all over. The ground just seemed to slip from under him and he fell, mouth and nose full of vomit. "It's knocked me out completely," he thought. Somebody took his arm. They dragged him 50 yards to the park in Vlajkoviceva Street. A woman put a damp piece of black cloth over his face. He couldn't breathe.

Zarko Korac had installed himself at the corner of Kosovska and Palmoticeva Streets. One minute the police were running past, the next the demonstrators. Then more police fled from the back door of the Parliament. A bare-headed policeman stopped in the middle of Palmoticeva Street. A young man grabbed his gun.

"Give it back to him," Korac shouted.

"Only because you say so, Professor," the young man said. "Only because of you."

The policeman stood there with his gun in his hand.

"What's this one doing?" thought Korac.

"They'll kill you here. They're going to lynch you," he said.

"Don't I know you?" the policeman said. He appeared to have no intention of going anywhere.

"For God's sake, they'll kill you!" shouted Korac. "Get out of here!"

"No," said the policeman, shaking his head. "I won't!"

There was an angry mob coming along Palmoticeva Street. Some of them were pushing garbage containers. The smell of the burning Parliament hung in the air. And in the middle of it the policeman, paralyzed, looked as if he were braced for revolutionary traffic control.

Just then an ambulance appeared from God knows where. Korac managed, without too much trouble, to bundle the policeman into it and the paramedics put him on the floor. He was still muttering "I won't, I won't," to himself. They slammed the door. "Get moving!" Korac shouted to the driver.

The flames leapt higher on Kosovska Street. Demonstrators appeared at the windows of the Parliament building. "A human life is no small thing," thought Korac. He headed off toward DOS headquarters, satisfied.

Palavestra came outside of the apartment building on Palmoticeva Street. Two vans exploded in Kosovska Street behind the Parliament. People were waving all sorts of things from the windows of the building, even chairs. Small groups were gathering around the burning cars. When the fire blazed up, they ran back, only to return when it subsided. Palavestra couldn't understand what they were looking for. He left for the square.

One battle was over. The revolutionary army was dragging its booty along Kosovska Street: cartons of cooking oil, mineral water, chairs, hat racks, paintings. The victors waved their trophies: shields and batons. Helmets once belonging to the police were now sitting at jaunty angles on the heads of the demonstrators.

EIGHTEEN

TEAR GAS FROM THE SKIES

Police Minister Stojiljkovic was in his office, dialing numbers and giving orders. On another line he was receiving instructions from Milosevic. He didn't go to the Ministry of Internal Affairs office, ten yards from his own. The police generals received their orders by telephone. The Parliament had already fallen when it occurred to him to use helicopters. The generals called the colonel in the green room.

"The order is to drop chemicals from the chopper, to disperse the crowds," he was told.

The colonel was ready. He didn't expect anything but lunatic orders that day. This one meant that tear-gas canisters, each weighing somewhere between 11 and 22 pounds, were to be dropped on the people. Even a coin, dropped from a few hundred yards, can kill before it hits the ground. "Somebody wants a massacre," he thought, as he drove toward the military airport at Batajnica.

He and another officer loaded containers into the helicopter and took off. There was a traffic jam above the city. The police Bell 212 helicopter and a military Gazelle passed each other near Batajnica. The chopper was coming from the center of the city, flying at low altitude. "Everybody wants to see what's going on," the colonel thought.

Minutes later he was mesmerized. "It was an amazing sight to see so many people," he said later. "Every street full of people, almost the whole of Belgrade packed."

"Who are we supposed to disperse?" he asked himself. "It's all over!"

Stanko Lazendic still didn't believe it. People were coming out of the Parliament, Kosovska Street was ablaze, and he still didn't know whether this was a victory. They were sure to come back, he thought, looking up at the sky. He had been startled by the sound of an engine. A blue-and-white police helicopter was hovering over the Parliament. "They're going to drop tear gas!" he realized, with no idea where the thought came from.

"There's a heavy smoke cover here," the colonel told headquarters. "We can't carry out the assignment." The demonstrators could be seen clearly on the ground. The colonel was shivering in his thin jacket.

"Go around again," ordered headquarters. The colonel obeyed. An hour later he was standing in front of his superiors.

"The conditions were unsuitable," he reported. They seemed relieved, he thought.

"Good," said one of the generals. "You may go."

This was just one of the extraordinary orders from Milosevic that Police Minister Stojiljkovic tried to obey on October 5.

Later the Serbian public was inundated with stories about orders that Milosevic had issued to the chief of staff of the Army, General Nebojsa Pavkovic: to dispatch the army to the Parliament; to send tanks to the RTS building; to cut transmission of the New RTS program; and to find, arrest, and probably execute 50 of the most prominent leaders and members of the opposition.

Zoran Djindjic, giving his account for this book, also claims that on October 5 Milosevic ordered the shelling of Beogradjanka, the building housing Studio B and other independent media.

"I spoke to Milosevic only after the developments around the Parliament and RTS," Pavkovic told the authors of this book. "He demanded that we separate the demonstrators and the police and seize the Parliament. I told him that the building had been abandoned by the police and the demonstrators were inside. He replied that the symbol of the state had been set on fire. 'It has been set on fire, but there are no casualties,' I told him. Later, there were other calls in connection with RTS. At that time the police reported casualties on both sides, saying they couldn't hold out and that it was a matter of urgency for the army to step in. I replied that the state was not under threat, that the constitutional order was not endangered and neither was the army. The orders I was receiving could not influence me to engage, or rather misuse, the army by supporting either side or any person in an attempt to influence the electoral will of the citizens. I wasn't prepared to carry out these orders."

Milosevic was surprised that the army didn't obey him, said Pavkovic.

"You didn't carry out a single one of my orders," Milosevic told him, without raising his voice.

"And thereby saved your face," thought Pavkovic.

Days later, Mira Markovic, the other half of the former first couple, accused Pavkovic of treason.

Pavkovic has also denied the claim that Milosevic had demanded the arrest of opposition leaders.

"There was a letter," said Pavkovic. "There were 40 names listed, not 50, and it was on State Security Service letterhead. If the letter had been from Milosevic he would certainly have asked me during the day whether the orders had been obeyed. He didn't. The General Staff was of the opinion that this was one more attempt to draw the army into the conflict."

Rade Markovic, the head of the State Security Service, speaking for this book, said that nobody, not even Milosevic, would ever have ordered anything of the sort. "In any case, if such a letter existed I would have seen it, and I have never received such an order." Markovic also denies the story about Milosevic ordering the shelling of Beogradjanka, the Studio B building, describing it as absurd. "Shelling Beogradjanka would mean that the missile would hit the building, three floors would be demolished and the missile would also hit the adjacent building, killing another 20 people. And why? Because of a demonstration? Even if somebody had issued such an order, who would have carried it out? There are experienced people at police headquarters, and they wouldn't pass such an order on."

The colonel from the green room also expressed doubts about the order to shell Beogradjanka. "It would have achieved nothing. After all, that's not the only television station, either in Belgrade or in the rest of Serbia."

These arguments of Milosevic's former associates are fairly convincing. On the other hand, was it any more rational to order an attack with Hornets on buses full of protesters, the "elimination" of the Kolubara miners, or an airdrop of tear-gas canisters?

The one clear fact emerging from October 5 is that none of what was contemplated, planned, or ordered was actually carried out. Despite that, Milosevic's face and honor weren't saved. The rest of the political establishment more or less scraped through.

NINETEEN

RESCUING THE POLICE

October 5, 4:40 P.M. Avala 45 to Avala 10: "I'm inside the building, the demonstrators are in front. I can't get out."

Avala 10: "Do you have contact with the unit?"

Avala 45: "No. I can't get through to them."

"I'm not from an occupying army!" Zarko Korac shouted at a group of police officers he found in front of Democratic Opposition of Serbia (DOS) headquarters at No. 3 Terazije. "Why are you surrendering to me?" He was as astonished as they were. But they were much more frightened. Then Ljiljana Lucic, a Democratic Party official, came down. "The building is full of police," she said. "They've come to surrender." "Good God!" exclaimed Korac. "What next?"

This was all the DOS needed. From the moment Velja Ilic rushed off to the Parliament on his own at noon, nothing had gone as planned. There'd been a problem of coordination throughout the afternoon. The Parliament had been seized without any of the DOS leaders giving the signal to attack. The burning of the Parliament hadn't been part of the plan, but it was now their responsibility nonetheless. Now they also needed to rescue the police. On the afternoon of October 5, without expecting it, the opposition leaders had become the government.

Nebojsa Covic had been a senior official in Milosevic's Socialist Party, so for him it was easy to pick up his old role. The others were in shock as they tried to get used to their new status. Korac recalls going into Covic's party headquarters and sitting with him and a nervous-looking Djindjic. He noticed a woman in the room: she seemed somehow familiar.

"Excuse me," said Korac. "Do I know you?"

"Zarko!" the astonished woman replied. "It's me, Ruzica!"

"I'd known Djindjic's wife for years," Korac recalled later. "I know her perfectly well, but at that moment I couldn't place her. I've never been under so much stress."

Covic was the first to make a plan. Democratic Opposition of Serbia people were sent to locate and protect the police. There were reports of many police officers in the entrances of residential buildings on Kosovska, Palmoticeva, and Vlajkoviceva Streets. There were many more in the Parliament and in the offices of nearby companies. Those who knew the location of the DOS party offices were the first to save themselves. Meanwhile, the DOS officials still on the streets were left to their own devices and did the best they could.

Sveta Djurdjevic, DOS's liaison with the police, gave his business card to any plainclothes officer he recognized, and there were a great many of them. From a truck in front of the Parliament, Velja Ilic roared: "They're on our side! Don't attack them. They'll all be on our side any minute now!" The residents of Kosovska Street and the surrounding area did what they could to help.

Aleksandar Blagojevic had to walk home the long way. People were beating police in Vlajkoviceva Street. The tear-gas cartridges fired from the police station on Majke Jevrosime Street were skimming the rooftops. His apartment on Kosovska Street, the same street where he now stood, was about fifty yards away, but now it seemed much farther. He had to walk down Nusiceva Street, along Lole Ribara Street, back up Palmoticeva Street, and on to Majke Jevrosime Street. From there he jumped a wall and crossed through a number of courtyards before reaching the back of his building. Along the way he collected a few people who, like himself, were weeping copiously, coughing their lungs out, and gasping for breath.

He hadn't seen his wife in the crowd. Marija Nedeljkovic was a member of the Keepers of the Flame, a group led by Ceda Jovanovic that had marched through the streets of Belgrade in protest every evening from September 21, 1999, to September 21, 2000. She had been with Mladjan Dinkic since the morning. When hell broke loose on Vlajkoviceva Street they had been only a few feet from each other, but he didn't know that. He had been in the street and she in the alley connecting Nikola Pasic Square with Kosovska Street through the Borba building and the Revolution Museum.

He took the whole lot back to his place. He told them to make themselves at home, freshen themselves up, and use the telephone. He felt the need to do a good turn for somebody that day. One guy from Obrenovac grabbed the phone. "Hello!" he shouted into the receiver. "It's started here. Move on to the police station straightaway! Straight away! Disarm the police! Disarm them!" This was serious stuff, thought Aleksandar. The whole third floor was shaking with the revolution.

The Obrenovac guy discovered Aleksandar's own police. Every now and then he peered through the peephole in the door. "They're here!" he exclaimed at one point. A hush fell over the room. Boots could be heard on the stairs. "It's the same every time," whispered Aleksandar. "They search our apartments after demonstrations."

The noise quickly died away. "They've gone," whispered the guy from Obrenovac. Aleksandar went outside to check. The man from Obrenovac and a couple of women left to set out for their homes. They bumped into the police on the ground floor. There were about 30 of them huddled on the stairs.

"Who do you belong to?" asked Aleksandar, looking them over. They looked like an army in disarray. Their gear was all over the place. They were sweating, messy, and frightened.

"We don't belong to anybody," several of them answered.

"That's obvious," thought Aleksandar. He was starting to feel sorry for them. "Do you want a drink?" he offered. They wanted to pay. No, said Aleksandar, the drinks were on him. Three policemen from Vranje accepted.

Marija ran in half an hour later with another policeman in tow. His wife was in labor, she said from the doorway, and demanded they give him the phone.

The household was in an uproar. Even more than it had been 14 months earlier when the Transfiguration Parliament, the first post-war opposition rally, had been broadcast on the Internet from their apartment. The police officers had found hospitality in the very place where, before that day, they would have been most unwelcome.

As the day wore into evening they repented, ate, and cheered up. The youngest of the officers, born in 1977 and wearing a flak jacket for the first time that day, told how their commander had sent them off from Vranje, wishing them good luck before he himself returned home. Between mouthfuls of food they told how they had been lucky to escape from the Parliament building by breaking down a door.

Aleksandar gave them civilian clothes to wear and led them out into the dark Belgrade night. They didn't know the streets, nor did they know where they had set off from. He took them to 29th November Street and pointed them to the Belgrade police headquarters. They left their gear and uniforms behind. The Blagojevic-Nedeljkovic apartment looked like a police quarter-master's store.

4:56 P.M. Avala 45 to Avala 10: "I've been given an ultimatum to surrender."

(In the background, at headquarters, someone mutters "What the fuck . . . !")

Avala 10: Roger.

Colonel Buha was trying to catch his breath. "Where are my men?" he thought. "Where are they?" There were eight policemen around him. "They're my men, too," he kept thinking. These men were mostly from the Belgrade riot squad. Some of them had been in Kosovo. "All right," he told them. "We'll go upstairs."

They climbed up several flights of stairs, to get as far as possible from the main entrance and the angry mob. Kosovska Street was already packed with people.

The building Buha was in was also packed. "Scum! Shame!" he heard people yelling behind as he ran up the stairs.

They faced an angry woman: "What on earth do you think you're doing? You should be ashamed of yourselves!"

Buha shrugged. "Please let us get through. We've had enough of it, too!"

Her face changed. She invited them in and left the door wide open. Buha waved in thanks. The police climbed another flight of stairs.

Slobodan Pajic knew the police didn't stand a chance. He'd been on the force for 16 years, until January 13, 2000, when Milosevic wanted to decorate him for his work in Kosovo. "And just what did I do there?" Pajic asked himself. "Ran off without doing my job." He refused the medal and quit.

On the afternoon of October 5 Pajic was head of security for Nebojsa Covic. He had been saying for a long time that the police stood no chance at all in clashes with the mob, and now he was seeing how right he had been. Covic let him go out into the streets and give a helping hand. Mostly he helped his former colleagues who were hiding in the lobbies of buildings and other secluded places, their faces smudged and beaten, stripped of their guns and gear and facing a lynch mob. He had no sympathy for them. "They should have used their heads," he told Covic. Then he went out again to help more. He eventually fought his way through the smoke to Kosovska Street. Democratic Opposition of Serbia security had told him eight policemen and their commander were holed up in No. 43.

There were already armed DOS teams in place outside the entrance to the building. Pajic and two of his men sneaked into the building.

"There are 150 or 200 of them," one policeman told Colonel Buha. He'd been sent down to the entrance to check the situation. "They have bandannas on their faces. Twenty of them have automatic rifles," the scout reported. Buha gripped his pistol. "What are they doing?" he asked.

"Just standing there, waiting," the man replied.

The Belgrade Police Brigade commander's head was throbbing. There was the staircase. "We have pistols and they have automatic rifles. There'll be people killed all over the place, including the residents here." He heard the front door open. Someone was creeping very quietly up the stairs.

Pajic was trying not to look nervous. The police commander was pale. "A brigade commander," Pajic recognized the insignia. "He's lost his unit. Gently . . . gently . . ." he told himself.

"Good afternoon," he said. "I'm Slobodan Pajic, a former colleague of yours."

"Buha," the officer replied.

5:00 P.M. Slobodan Pajic to Avala 10: "My name is Pajic. I have one of your units here. They are not willing to use force against the people. Please don't start another bloodbath."

Avala 10: "Get off the air. Don't interfere with this job."

Pajic: "Pull your units out. Do you want them lynched?"

Avala 10: "Stop interfering."

Colonel Buha wanted to speak to the opposition leaders. Pajic had nothing against that. Covic was the first to arrive for a series of meetings with the trapped policemen. He said later that he would never forget it. He spoke to the deeply distressed young men, some of whom were in tears. Buha wanted his men spared. That was all he was concerned about. He refused to surrender himself. "If you need a dead commander," he told Covic, "I have no problem with that."

"No way!" said Covic. They agreed that Colonel Buha should stay in one of the apartments. This turned out to be one of the most critical meetings for the future of the revolution.

5:03 P.M. Avala 1441 to Avala 10: "Avala 10, do you read me?"

Avala 10: "Roger. Where are you located?"

Avala 1441: "In the building."

Avala 10: "In the Parliament building?"

Avala 1441: "That is correct."

Avala 10: "Are you able to take action?"

Avala 1441: "I'm here with Cedomir Jovanovic. We're surrounded by his men. Are you able to contact these people? So that we know how to proceed?"

Ceda had regained consciousness with counterattack on his mind. "We've broken them," he thought, as he looked at the Parliament. "There are no more of them. But what if they come back?" He began shouting "Close in on the Parliament. Close in on it! Guard it!" and stormed into the building. The fire was raging on every side.

Ceda ran into a man carrying a telephone. Then another one dragging a painting. Someone ran past with a hat stand over his shoulder. Someone else told him that there were still police in the Chamber of the Citizens. Ceda went in and slowly closed the door behind him. The guys following him stayed outside.

"Who's in charge here?" he barked. There was silence in the chamber.

"Who's in charge here. Fuck you. Give me someone to talk to. Are you all dumb?"

One officer stepped forward. "I'm the commander here. Unit 1441."

The hall was full of smoke. The commander wiped his eyes. Ceda's stomach was churning. He threw his arms around the commander and hugged him. The man was shaking like a leaf.

"It's going to be all right, man," said Ceda. "Everything's going to be all right. It's not worth it. It's all over now, you understand? It's all over!"

"All over. It's all over," the commander repeated, robot-like. "I understand, it's all over."

Then the commander of Unit 1441 called headquarters on his walkie-talkie.

5:04 P.M. Avala 10 to Avala 1441: "Are you able to take action?"

Avala 1441: "No, I can't. I'm surrounded."

Avala 10: "Stay in position, 1441. Stay put."

Avala 1441: "I need to speak to my superior."

Avala 10: "I'm your commanding officer!"

Avala 1441: "I need the one who sent me here."

The commander switched off his walkie-talkie. "All right," he said, curtly. "We surrender." A wave of relief swept over Ceda.

"This must be the maximum–minimum under the laws of probability," thought Anclave Clinic director Slobodan Ivanovic. The Parliament was ablaze, people were celebrating all around him and he still hadn't seen any serious injuries. His only patients so far had been two protesters wearing flak jackets who were unable to breathe. He'd intubated them with a plastic airway to prevent them from choking and given them oxygen for 45 minutes, after which they were able to walk away.

It looked to Ivanovic as if he'd have nothing to do all afternoon. Then the Borba situation began to develop.

Two muscular young men with cropped hair, wearing jackets, arrived. One said they had a patient for him and pointed to the Borba building. Ivanovic picked up his bag and went with them.

The patient's name was Dusan Cukic. He was one of the most notorious journalists of the Milosevic regime, the editor in chief of *Vecernje novosti*. He had spacious offices in the Radio Television Serbia building stuffed with Socialist Party propaganda, and he had a broad range of clandestine responsibilities. Now he was on the verge of a heart attack. Ivanovic found him on the ground floor, hiding at the back of the security booth. He could neither stand nor speak.

"I'd be the same, in his position," thought Ivanovic. He sedated the man. Outside the Borba building, protesters were howling "Come on out, Cukic. We want to shoot you dead!" Cukic was ashen, cold and sweating.

"He's had it," thought Ivanovic. The three men removed Cukic's distinctive eyeglasses and put a hood over his head. Ivanovic drove the Anlave Clinic's Mercedes ambulance to the main entrance of the building. They bundled Cukic, bent over between two bodyguards, into the ambulance.

Ivanovic returned to his field hospital. "Fuck," he thought. "That was a close call." One of the Borba security guards returned. It wasn't over. In fact it was getting more complicated.

"Doctor," said the guard, "We've got 25 policemen in the boiler room. You're an intellectual. Please, tell us what we should do with them."

Ivanovic picked up his bag again.

Back in the building he didn't waste time on explanations.

"Strip down to your underwear, all of you," he said as he walked through the door. "Put your uniforms and your weapons in the lockers. Take some ordinary workmen's uniforms and get out of here. And be careful. If they get a whiff of who you are they'll kill you!"

All but two of the police followed his advice. He helped them leave through the back of the building.

TWENTY

MILANOVIC RUNS THE GAUNTLET

In June 1990, only months after the first opposition political party was established in Serbia, novelist Borislav Pekic took several blows from a police officer's baton outside the RTS building at No. 10 Takovska Street.

The elderly author took it in his stride. He even joked about the blows to his legs with the rubber truncheon. "They're used to it," he said. "The Communists were beating them 40 years ago!"

Not long afterward, Pekic died. Perhaps not from that beating, but as a result of all the beatings and imprisonment he had endured during his life. Probably his dream of a country where justice prevailed was no more important to him than his other longings, but the authorities saw him as a man obsessed, and that was his misfortune.

Radio Television Serbia and the police baton survived through June of 1990 and became the powerful twin symbols of the regime of one man and, as time went on, of his family. Radio Television Serbia propped up the truncheon, and the truncheon underpinned and defended the RTS. They couldn't do without each other, and Milosevic could do without neither. His entire relationship with the people he led, and who had quickly tired of him, was based on the electronic box of RTS he had invaded in the early 1990s. He was never seen anywhere else: he didn't go to sporting events or concerts; he didn't walk around the city; he didn't go shopping. He lived only on and from the television screen.

The lie cooked up at No. 10 Takovska Street and aired on the prime-time national television news reached 3.5 million homes in Serbia. It was the most valuable of all the lies he came up with during his 13-year reign.

For this lie he was prepared to risk everything. This was demonstrated soon after Pekic was beaten. On March 9, 1991, one protester and one policeman lost their lives in demonstrations against the state television. The man who spearheaded the protests was Vuk Draskovic, the leader of the Serbian Renewal Movement and the undisputed king of the streets in those days. Human life, even the lives of the police he used as pawns, mattered less to Milosevic than did RTS. With the support of the state television he "won" elections, lost wars in Croatia, Bosnia, and Kosovo, and yet he reigned on. The police baton took care of everything else.

Radio Television Serbia was dubbed TV Bastille after these events. The smell of revolution was in the air even then, and the alienated dictator and the symbols of his rule had no alternative but to rely on the state media. Vuk Draskovic didn't succeed, and the television became more and more an object of hatred. In the protests of 1996 and 1997, people threw eggs at it. In April 1999, when it was struck by NATO bombs, graffiti appeared on the adjacent Russian Orthodox Church: "See, Vuk, this is how to storm the Bastille!"

The callousness of this message, given that 16 employees of Radio Television Serbia had been killed in the bombing, didn't change the fact that many people would have been happy to see Milosevic's media fortress razed. Zoran Djindjic, recalling those events for this book, said that in polls taken before the demonstrations many opposition supporters from outside Belgrade said they were coming to Belgrade mainly to destroy TV Bastille. On October 5, they swept into Belgrade once more. They finished the job and the Parliament and moved on to TV Bastille. Draskovic wasn't there to lead them. They didn't care. They didn't need him. But the man who renamed the state media will be remembered for this, among other things. By dubbing Radio Television Serbia "TV Bastille," Draskovic defined both its true nature as a fortress, and the way to get rid of it: revolution. He was right on both counts.

The name "Bastille" brings up another important detail: when revolutions begin, the prisons are usually empty, with no one to defend them. When RTS came under attack, 80 percent of the Serbian population no longer had any faith in it, which was tantamount to it being deserted. The truncheon, already abused and defeated in the storming of the Parliament, now couldn't even be raised.

Novelist Borislav Pekic must have been laughing from the grave as his vendetta marched on down Takovska Street.

✦✦ ✦✦ ✦✦

4:23 P.M. Officer at RTS to Avala 10: "Heavy pressure on the television. I've repelled the first assault."

Avala 10: "Follow your orders."

Miodrag Zupanc, the RTS school programs editor, was listening to the trumpeters in front of No. 10 Takovska Street. A hundred yards up the road there was a war going on. The trumpets announced it. Fifty or so police ran across Majke Jevrosime Street into the RTS building. Three of them were trying to hide the rattles protruding from the pockets of their uniforms. The rattle had been the most popular toy in Belgrade for days. It was the death rattle for Milosevic.

Zupanc believed that things might end well after all. A few minutes later, when two guys armed with bricks ran past, toward the television building, he tried to stop them. "Don't do that!" he shouted. The windows shattered. "Please, don't!" he pleaded again. The first tear-gas cartridges were fired from the building. The protesters ran off.

4.27 P.M. Avala 10 to unidentified officer: "What's your location?"

Officer: "Revolution Boulevard, near the Metropol hotel."

Avala 10: "Proceed to the television."

Avala 10, to another unidentified officer: "What's your location?"

Officer: "Near the Vuk Karadzic monument."

Avala 10: "Proceed to the television."

First officer: "I can't get through!"

Avala 10: "Take your men out of the vehicles. Get to the television building fast. Use chemicals to remove any obstruction."

Rade Veljanovski wasn't fleeing the revolution, he was fleeing the tear gas. He and his associate, Nada Kovacevic, from the Peace and Crisis Management Foundation, passed through the whole of central Belgrade. From the Parliament across Terazije Square to Narodnog Fronta Street, then through Brankova Street to Carice Milice Street, and eventually to Lole Ribara Street. They ran across Takovska Street, which was heavy with tear gas. Then they ran directly into the police. Ilije Garasanina Street was swarming with blue uniforms. There were three personnel carriers in front of the old Cepelin disco and three buses parked on the street itself, near the high school. There were police everywhere, inside and outside the building.

Ilije Garasanina Street is behind the television building. From it, the narrow Aberdareva Street leads to the newer section of the massive RTS headquarters. The state media premises is in three sections: one brand new, all glass and sharp angles, the other two older, in the social realism style. The larger of these is on Takovska Street and the smaller on Aberdareva Street. The three interconnected buildings have a total of four entrances: one from Takovska Street and three from Aberdareva Street. Whichever entry is used, the winding corridors eventually lead to everywhere in the three buildings. Ilije Garasanina Street and Tasmajdan Park have traditionally been the holding points for police reinforcements during demonstrations outside RTS.

Nada Kovacevic cracked. "Aren't you ashamed of yourselves?" she screamed at the police. "What are you doing here?" she shouted, straight into their faces. The astonished police were silent. Rade and Nada crossed the long line of police buses, four-wheel-drives, vans, and police officers stretching along both sides of Garasanina Street all the way to Starine Novaka Street, which opens onto Revolution Boulevard, splitting the vast Tasmajdan Park in two.

The chaos had begun. Two cordons of police officers were coming along the street, firing tear gas in all directions. To Rade, the police officers looked more like a mob than an organized force. Two police buses followed slowly, close behind the cordons. They looked like an irresistible force ready to sweep the entire street in one pass.

Rade and Nada ran across the street, entering Tasmajdan Park behind the law school. Then it dawned on them. The police were trying to retreat. They were being pelted with stones, bottles, bricks, even pieces of wood torn from the benches lining the park. Tasmajdan was bursting with protesters. There was no safe haven for the police in central Belgrade that day.

The police were also under attack a few hundred yards away, at the corner of Starine Novaka and 27th March Streets. Bands of angry people were taking cover behind the garbage containers, buses, and cars that were serving as roadblocks on the street, hurling whatever was at hand at the police.

It was starting to look like a Western. Two police buses flanked the police cordon. They were surrounded, everywhere, by Belgraders, who were screaming like wild animals. The police, huddled between the two buses, ran to Belgrade police headquarters on 29th November Street. "Victory!" roared the mob.

4:33 P.M. Unidentified officer at the RTS building to Avala 10: "We're following orders but we can't hold out much longer."

Avala 10: "Fire a few shots over their heads. Take further action!"

One Belgrade police officer, sitting in his office three floors below, heard this order on the police radio. He changed out of his uniform, told his colleagues: "Fuck you all. I'm not having anything to do with this," and left the building.

The colonel from the green room, who later played back the recordings of all radio communications that day, said that "further action" meant only one thing: firing directly at the protesters.

They'd been firing for some time when President of the Civil Alliance of Serbia Goran Svilanovic came up Takovska Street to the RTS building. The street was filled with smoke from tear gas cartridges. People were kicking at the cartridges, which emitted a hissing sound when they hit the ground. There were large rubber bullets flying past. Part of the building facing Kakovska Street was already ablaze, the burning curtains flapping through the broken windows.

The police were trapped and making a last-ditch effort to defend themselves in the glass entrance hall. The demonstrators ran at them, throwing stones and Molotov cocktails. One was even brandishing a fire extinguisher. Svilanovic, true to the name of his party, tried to remain calm and dignified. His conduct seemed surreal. Snatching the fire extinguisher from the man wielding it, he approached the window and tried to put out the fire. One small man against a roaring blaze. The revolutionaries around him were astounded. "Are you insane?" one of them screamed.

Another one recognized him: "Come on Svilanovic, knock it off. What are you doing? We'll just light it again. Let it burn!"

Dwarfed by the blaze, Svilanovic finally realized how futile his efforts were. He threw the extinguisher away. At that moment, roaring and shrieking, a bulldozer lumbered down Takovska Street.

4.40 P.M. Unidentified officer to Avala 10: "Action not effective."

Avala 10: "Continue action! Continue!"

Officer: "There's a bulldozer at the door! It's barring access. There's no one to back me up."

Avala 10: "Take the logical action: Do what I told you!"

Joe drove straight into the television building four times at full speed. He sounded the horn, put the engine into gear and rammed straight into the main entrance. The police huddled inside responded with a salvo of tear gas. The cartridges ricocheted off the massive scoop and the driver's cab. The bulldozer reversed.

Joe was choking from the smoke. He thought he was going to die. The old man beside him was wearing a gas mask he had gotten from one of the protesters. He sat like a statue. Joe honked again. One young demonstrator climbed up next to the cab. "Go for it!" he yelled. "Let them fire everything they've got, fuck them!"

Before his third assault, Joe flattened the iron bumper posts that surrounded the parking lot in front of the main entrance. The revolutionary army took them up as weapons. The third assault was a joint effort. Joe was getting sick of the to and fro. "Now," he told himself, "let's show them that Joe means business!" The bulldozer screamed. The scoop tore into the left side of the entrance. One of the steel ribs propping up the roof over the vestibule was left leaning at an odd angle.

Maki saw a tall policeman waving a handgun. He was hugging the wall of the television building, close to the main entrance. From time to time he would aim and fire the gun. Maki realized he was firing into the mob. This was what he had expected all along. Claw to claw. It was savage, brutal, he kept thinking to himself. He didn't waste any time. "I thought about sending someone to kill him," he said later, giving his account for this book. "Literally. I meant it! To kill him! It was us or them. We were at each other's throats. Like animals!"

His men were ready for action. They even had a gun. Seized from some anonymous policeman in the Parliament, it was now a revolutionary weapon.

Fortunately, this revolution was full of surprises. It happened in flashes, unrelated, and changing direction, almost in the blink of an eye. When Maki blinked, the policeman had gone. The unraveling sequence of events had saved his life. Maki turned his head. There were shots coming from all directions.

Gigo ran down Takovska Street. He didn't want to watch the looting of the Parliament. He had more urgent business to attend to. The street was full of smoke. Smoking cartridges were ricocheting off the ground. He recognized the building on fire to his right. Thousands of people were pouring down Takovska Street toward it. Shots rang out. The guy next to Gigo crashed to the ground as though someone had tripped him as he ran. Blood had been spilt in Takovska Street. Gigo knew it straightaway. The dark stain was spreading on the man's trouser leg. He had been wounded in the thigh, a few inches from the groin, and he was holding tightly to the wound. Gigo tried in vain to stem the flow of blood with the bandanna he had been wearing across his face. "This man's wounded!" he shouted. "Get an ambulance!" And then, seemingly out of nowhere, an ambulance came.

"Smash it! Smash it!" shouted the old man next to Joe. But Joe couldn't do it. The cab was full of tear gas. In any case he was more interested in forcing the enemy to surrender than in destroying anything. "Every single one of them," he thought, as he shifted into reverse.

A gas mask landed in the cab. Someone in front of the bulldozer told him to put it on. Joe honked again. Now fully equipped, he drove into the thickest part of the smoke. He lowered the scoop. "I crashed in!" said Joe later. "There was glass breaking, everything falling around and I could see them running away. The old man shouted to the mob: "Get in there! Get in! The television has been liberated!" The protesters rushed in. Joe noticed all of them were carrying a rock in each hand. "They'll beat them now!" he thought.

From the main entrance someone yelled: "Don't do it, guys! Not Serb against Serb!"

"Listen to that," thought Joe, honking persistently. "Not Serb against Serb! Then what was going on until a moment ago?" There were two holes in the windscreen of the cab. One was right at head height. His jacket, draped over the seat, was shot through. "Fuck me!" thought Joe. "That was a close call." The design of his bulldozer had saved his life. The cab of the International 538 rotates together with the scoop. Had it been fixed, as on all other bulldozers, he would have been dead. He felt no sympathy for the police when the protesters began beating them.

4:49 P.M. Unidentified officer to Avala 10: "I'm in the middle of the mob. Surrounded!"

The events at the television building came closest to following the DOS scenario, mostly because the building, right in the center of Belgrade, had been completely cut off. Groups of demonstrators had done an excellent job on all the roads leading to RTS, and on a very wide diameter. Every route that gave access to the building from Roosevelt Street, Revolution Boulevard, 27th March and Beogradska Streets, and Slavija Square from the south, west, and north had been cut off. The west had already been cut off with the storming of the Parliament. Roadblocks had been set up on access roads to central Belgrade. The protesters, armed with Molotov cocktails and far more lethal weapons, had taken up positions along the roads to the outer residential areas of Banjica, Cukarica, and Pancevo, which could have been used to move troops from their barracks. Wasps were again the weapon of choice. But this time they were in the hands of the protesters.

The rest of the job around the television building was carried out by unorganized groups of enraged citizens. They were following nobody's command.

A tear-gas cartridge whistled past Marko's head. It had been fired at the Delije from a few yards away as they pushed through the main door. "There you are, you have a new birthday," one of his friends from the pit said as they beat a retreat toward the steps up to Dusko Radovic Theatre and Tasmajdan Park.

Marko was vomiting every 15 minutes. His stomach had long been empty, but he continued to retch and spit. Then they saw the bulldozer in action. The entrance of the television caved in. Ivan threw away his club, the traditional weapon of the Red Star fans and ran, unarmed, to the door. The scenes from the Parliament were being repeated: the police were stripped of their gear and some of them beaten brutally. The Delije didn't want to waste their time on this. They rushed for the stairs. That was the way to Aberdareva Street, where the real war was still raging.

One policeman was moving slowly along the wall toward the stairs. His helmet was gone but his gas mask was still in place, and he still had his gun. Ivan was at the stairs before he saw him. He turned toward the policeman without fear. A second later it was all over for the Red Star fan, the guy from the northern stand of the stadium. The policeman aimed. Ivan stared blankly. He distinctly heard one shot, then another. He fell to the ground and knew in that instant that he had been hit. The burning pain in his leg seemed somehow familiar, although he'd never been shot before. "I fell and then immediately stood up again," said Ivan later. "I thought I'd better stand up because if I lay there, nobody would notice. So I stood up and ran." He fell onto Marko. "I've been shot," he said, and collapsed.

4:55 P.M. Field unit at RTS to Avala 10: "They're using firearms against us! We need back-up at once!"

(In the background, someone says "Fuck those bastards!")

Avala 10: "You have to hold out!"

Rade and Nada heard the shots and ran for cover. They chose the wrong direction. The mob fleeing the television building through the park and past the Last Chance café pressed forward. The tear-gas cartridges caught up with them. Rade and Nada, not quite knowing why, elbowed their way on toward the RTS building. They took cover behind tree trunks from the whistling cartridges. Then they hurried past the café and ducked behind the fence. Someone shouted at them to get down because of the shooting.

Twenty-odd yards below the tight curve in the path at the edge of the park was the RTS parking lot on Aberdareva Street.

4:57 P.M. Unidentified officer to Avala 10: "There's a strong push from Aberdareva Street. They're throwing Molotov cocktails!"

Avala 10: "Roger."

Milan Lazendic saw it all from the steps. He'd just arrived from Takovska Street, almost at a stroll. Rade, watching from above in Aberdareva Street, saw the same scene. A handful of guys no older than 17 were throwing stones and bottles plugged with burning rags at the building and at the Aberdareva Street parking lot. Ten or so cars caught fire. One of the boys crept over to a white Lada, climbed in, and soon had the engine running. As he rammed the burning vehicles, pushing them around the parking lot, Rade realized what he was doing. "He's trying to block the entrance. They'll be burned alive!"

4:58 P.M. Unidentified officer to Avala 10: "It's impossible to repel the assault. Any more chemicals available?"

Avala 10: "Hold out just a little longer. Backup's on the way. They're outside the building."

"The army will come." That's what two policemen told the RTS news staff assembled on the third floor of the new glass-and-steel building in Aberdareva Street at 4 o'clock.

"They told us not to panic," Juliana Jovanovic said later. "That's why we stayed until the last moment."

The third floor housed the newsroom, the typing pool, the offices for the duty staff, the media library, and offices for the business and domestic correspondents, the assistant editor in chief, the current affairs editor, and the program producer. The editor in chief, along with the editor and director of the foreign desk, had offices on the fourth floor. These offices were separated from the other buildings on Aberdareva and Takovska Streets by a heavy steel fire door. The newsroom looked out on the Fifth Belgrade Comprehensive School and the Palilula Market. The staff were somewhat cocooned inside. They were unaware of what was going on outside until that side of the building went up in flames. The alarm was raised by cooks running down from the fifth floor, which was already ablaze. "Fire!" they shouted. The newsroom staff gave them milk to drink. Dusan Vojvodic calmed them down. This journalist, who had been promoted to the military rank of general by Milosevic, told them that the army was on the way and that the effects of tear gas lasted only 15 minutes.

Juliana's son telephoned. She told him that everything was all right and that he shouldn't worry. They had security guards. Everything was under control. As she put the phone down she thought, "I'll be burnt alive here, and the kids won't even have a body to bury!"

By now, everyone on the third floor knew that they were trapped. The tapes prepared for "News at Five" were put back on the shelf. They were choking on the tear gas. There were gunshots on Aberdareva Street.

5:00 P.M. Unidentified officer to Avala 10: "They've entered the building!"

Avala 10: "Why the hell don't you take action!"

Officer: "We're out of chemicals!"

Avala 10: "You'd better keep your voice down!"

A couple of confused policemen came out of the glass building through a construction entrance. The crowd that had gathered in the parking lot, on the stairs, and in Tasmajdan Park let out a roar of victory, or rather a scream. They booed the police, who immediately put their hands in the air. To Rade, from his vantage point up in Aberdareva Street, they looked like men who had been defeated long before this battle. "They're all fed up with it," he thought as he watched the protestors clap them on the shoulder and snatch their gear before letting the officers through to Garasanina Street. A few men were pushing at the locked door opening onto Aberdareva Street. Rade climbed down. He picked up a piece of wood, short but stout. The door cracked open.

5:10 P.M. Unidentified officer to Avala 10: "It's a very difficult situation here. They're advancing. The police are laying down their weapons!"

Avala 10: "Hold on for another two minutes. Backup's on the way."

Unidentified demonstrator speaking into a police walkie-talkie: "No one's going to help you!"

Juliana already had her coat on and her bag in hand when a man stormed into the office on the third floor just after 5 P.M.

"Get out!" he shouted.

In the newsroom she joined RTS staff members Ljiljana Milanovic, Staka Novovic, Spomenka Jovic, Lidija Radulovic, Vera Rajcevic, Dragan Vukelic, Ruzica Vranjkovic, Rajko Rakicevic, Sonja Djuric, Sasa Barbulovic, and Dusan Vojvodic. They all obeyed in silence. One of the editing assistants attempted to hide in a closet. Juliana Jovanovic was among the last to leave, holding hands with Sonja Djuric.

Milan ran into the building through the same entrance the police had come out of. Rade, clutching his makeshift club, hurried along the hallway and into the glass section of the building. Milan came across the RTS people on the staircase. Rade found them too.

The revenge began.

"They looked hideous," Juliana said later. The group from the office was escorted to the stairs. "I'm sure they weren't Belgraders," she added.

There were people lined up, waiting for them. Sasa Barbulovic raised his hands. Someone shouted out to leave the women alone. Sasa's head swung around. They punched them and kicked them and beat them with crowbars. One of them looked Juliana straight in the eye, screaming at her that she was Milosevic's whore.

A man in a police uniform stood on the landing between the second and third floors. He shouted at them: "Why the fuck did you stay here this long? To die, for the sake of one man!" No one touched Juliana. The others all felt the sting of ugly, brutal, ruthless human rage.

Rade, club in hand, stood at the foot of the stairs between the second and third floors. Milanovic, the hated RTS director-general, came down first, in his blue shirtsleeves and gray trousers. Lidija Radulovic was behind him. "So this is what it's like when the Democrats take over," she said to Rade. He didn't reply, but ran after them.

Milan saw Milanovic fall down the stairs. He also saw Spomenka Jovic, terrified and bent over, being kicked and punched. On the fourth floor they beat a squirming policeman with iron bars. He was screaming with pain.

"You shot at us!" shouted the men with the bars. "You shot at us, you motherfucker!" They kept on thrashing him.

Milan Lazendic ran down the stairs. The policeman was still screaming. A man covered with a blanket was escorted out of the building by two others.

Milder came running through the main door. He was stripped to the waist, with a helmet, shield, and baton. He rushed along the corridors. Two guys from Sabac knew the way. They threaded their way through the maze of the fourth floor. In one of the many corridors they ran into Milorad Komrakov, the RTS editor in chief. The mob had already shoved him around. He was whimpering: "Please, please don't hurt me!"

Later, Milder thought he had made a mistake, but at the time he simply couldn't hit the man. There was something in the eyes of the hysterical editor, something in the whole business that made him pity the man.

He put the helmet on Komrakov's head. "Protect me," Komrakov pleaded. Someone brought a blanket. "Don't hurt me," he begged. They covered him with the blanket and took him out like that. The guys from Sabac were holding him by the arms. The scowling Milder led the way, shielding them from the crowd. They got all the way to the Belgrade City Assembly without anyone recognizing him.

5:30 P.M. Avala 10 to unidentified officer: "If you can't defend the building, pull the unit out."

For some time it was believed that Milanovic had been killed in the assault on the RTS building. Rade thought the story was true. So did Nada. She had been in the parking lot when the RTS journalists and editors came out of the construction entrance. She was in the front line of the seething, furious mob that beat, cursed, and spat at Juliana and the others as they passed through, bruised, humiliated, and scared stiff.

Staka Novovic was the only one who held her head high. And she suffered for it. She didn't head for the Fifth Comprehensive School, where she might have escaped her pursuers, but for Tasmajdan Park, teeming with more and more people every minute.

Nada chased after her. "I have no idea what came over me," she said later. "I saw her clutching a shopping bag with some food or something in it and screamed at her to hand it over."

She never found out what was in the bag. Staka Novovic hung on to it. "No!" she said. Nada lifted her umbrella to strike her. Staka fell into a pile of sand from the construction site. The mob descended on her.

"They didn't beat her," Nada said later. They threw sand over her and spat at her. Nada backed away. Radio Television Serbia's star news anchor sat in the sand, clutching her shopping bag and sobbing.

At about the same time, Milanovic dashed out of the old building in Aberdareva Street. He made it only a few steps before he stumbled and fell. The mob surrounded him. He screamed.

Rade was less than ten feet away. He was amazed to see the chief executive of RTS "bounce off the ground," as he put it later. Milanovic managed to flee, but also instead of heading for the Fifth Comprehensive School, he headed for the construction entrance of the glass building, straight into the mob.

The mob opened to receive him. Milanovic stopped, disoriented. The mob closed around him. Rade thought he was a goner. When he heard the howling he was sure of it.

Juliana eventually reached the school. Someone was shouting after her: "You fucking bitch! You've been lying to us for ten years." She fled past the Palilula market through back streets to the Dorcol area where she lived. Once home, she locked the door behind her and burst into tears. Then she knocked back three glasses of slivovitz.

It didn't help.

TWENTY-ONE

THE "BOYS FROM BRAZIL"

5:35 P.M. Unidentified voice: "Let me through. I should be there with my team."

Avala 10 to an officer in the RTS building: "The 'Boys from Brazil' have arrived."

This was a crucial moment for Zoran Djindjic. And for Milosevic. The only difference was that the leader of the Democratic Party knew what was happening. At least he hoped he did. When the "hammers," the special operations units of the Serbian State Security forces, roared out of their base located in the town of Banjica, no one could have guessed how it would end. As they screamed through the streets toward the television building, the main players could only pray. Milosevic was praying that his Praetorian Guard would make a triumphant counterstrike. Djindjic, on the other hand, was praying that their commander, Legija, would keep his word.

Legija was in the lead vehicle. His men, in combat uniforms and wearing gas masks, stood in the back of the armored vehicles. Gun barrels protruded from the carriers. The "Boys from Brazil" weren't the least bit nervous. They were used to nasty situations. Their job, as they said themselves, was to clean up the messes nobody else would.

The first time they came under fire that day was at the Slavija Street traffic circle. An old man hiding behind a garbage container fired nine rounds at them. Four shots hit the armor plating of the second vehicle in the convoy. They were also shot at on Beogradska Street and all the way down to the television building. They were hit 29 times in all.

"Fucking hell, what a lunatic nation!" thought one of the Praetorians, not without a hint of respect and some pride. He'd already seen his cousin in the mob, along with plenty of comrades-in-arms, now back in civilian clothes after Milosevic's wars. He was glad that the other Praetorians were cool. They didn't react to the bullets, or to the four flowerpots that landed on their helmets. A large rock almost broke the armor glass windshield of Legija's jeep.

The "hammers" roared onto Takovska Street, drowning out the noise of the mob. The sound made Maki's blood ran cold. He swore, thinking about tanks, about the special anti-terrorist squads, "Frankie's Guys." A friend of his, a black market dealer, pulled him out of the way. Everybody started to run. When he finally caught a glimpse of an armored vehicle, there was no doubt in Maki's mind.

"Dear God, we're all finished. They'll shoot us all like rabbits!" Speaking about it later for this book he said, "It gave me one hell of a fright!"

Joe was scared of these guys, too. He'd never seen anything like them in his life. The "hammers" screeched to a halt in front of the television building. "I thought they were going to jump out and get me," he explained later. As if in a dream, Joe saw the guys in the jeeps take off their masks and raise three fingers in the Serbian victory salute. The people swarmed over to them.

What actually happened outside the RTS building? Rade Markovic said later that he had dispatched his crack police units to the Parliament. The Ministry of Internal Affairs had received information that the police officers trapped inside the building were in danger and that they had been shot at. It all began to look like a military operation.

"I gave the order to rescue them," said Markovic. "They arrived at the Parliament and saw there were no longer any police there. The Parliament was in flames, and the situation they had been sent for no longer existed. They halted there, however. Their commander told me they'd come under fire and asked for new orders, so I told him to withdraw. I meant without the use of arms, of course, although I didn't say so, and he didn't ask. The commander played the pivotal role. He stepped out of the vehicle they were firing at, jumped onto the bonnet, and removed his mask. The people recognized, him, Legija, and started calling his name. He said to them, 'What's this all about, brothers? Why don't you stop shooting?' and gave the three-finger salute. In this way he neither surrendered nor put any lives at risk. He had recognized that there was no longer a job to do."

That's the official story.

The facts, of course, are different. On the police band, Avala 10 mentioned the "Boys from Brazil" only in reference to the television building.

The special operations units hadn't been mentioned once during the whole assault on the Parliament. The Parliament fell at 4:09 P.M. At 4:17, the Belgrade police chief, Milos Vojinovic, from command center Avala 10, directed all commanders to pull their men out of the Parliament.

Bosko Buha, the commander of the Police Brigade, spoke to Legija the next day. He says that the commander of the special operations unit, seeing what was happening at the television building, called police headquarters and told them they were insane. "Then Legija received a phone call from Milosevic himself and from that point on the former president's link to the police was broken. In the presence of one of my men who were guarding those vehicles of his, he threw his mobile or his walkie-talkie, whatever he was using, down and smashed it to pieces."

Maki felt great relief when he saw the men's three-fingered salute. "The army's on our side," he shouted. The "hammers" used the footpaths to roll down Revolution Boulevard. At the corner of Takovska and Kosovska Streets, they took protester Vladislav Trsek by surprise. He was rooted to the spot. "Whew," he exclaimed, "if they'd hit us with those we would have broken up hours ago!"

The whole ritual of making peace between "Frankie's Guys" and the mob was repeated in the Boulevard. All the way to Slavija Square and back to the Banjica base there were protesters hanging on the running boards of the vehicles.

Half an hour later, on Dobrinjska Street near the Serbian Parliament building, Zoran Djindjic climbed into an armored vehicle.

This time, Legija was alone, wearing his camouflage uniform and a flak jacket, with two handguns at his chest. "As far as I'm concerned," said the commander of "Frankie's Guys," "this business is over. Milosevic is out. There's no going back, the people have won themselves a victory."

Djindjic was satisfied. He was even more so when he inquired about the army. "I have heard that they're planning to intervene," he said.

Legija was convincing: "I'll let them know that if they intervene, we'll intervene against them. I have twelve hundred men."

"Your word?" Djindjic repeated the ritual of the night before.

"My word," said Legija curtly.

Once the Special Operations Units were out of the game, the battle for the television station was over. At 5:45 P.M. Avala 10 ordered the remaining police to withdraw to the base.

At the same time, Bubac met Misa Cumuras from Bubutovac. He was waving a hose and shouting "I thrashed the shit out of Sima Gajina."

Gigo was standing on Takovska Street, watching the fire.

Milder was handing Milorad Komrakov over to the DOS security guys at the Belgrade City Assembly.

Rade Veljanovski was at the Media Center shouting "The television has been liberated!"

Milan Lazendic found his brother.

Minister of Tourism Slobodan Cerovic had finally got some information. At the Yugoslav Left Directorate, after several unsuccessful attempts to get through, they told him that the television had fallen. "He's finished," thought Cerovic, and put the phone down.

Ivan Nikolic was on the operating table. He had been shot through the right thigh and the bullet had torn the main artery. He was already unconscious when Marko and the rest of the Delije brought him to the Madera restaurant in Tasmajdan Park. He lost two and a half litres of blood before he reached the hospital.

At the Red Star stadium, Ivan was known as "The Jinx." Three off-duty doctors from the Institute for Cardiovascular Surgery, Lazar Davidovic, Dusan Kostic, and Petar Stojanovic, who happened to be at the Madera that day, thought the nickname was inappropriate. With a wound like Ivan's, people usually die within ten minutes without proper medical assistance.

After the battles for the Parliament and the television building, 107 people sought medical assistance at the emergency medical center. Five had gunshot wounds: Ivan Nikolic, Dragan Matovic, Dusan Markovic, Bogdan Jovanovic, and Drasko Mitrovic. Cedomir Kalinic had burns on his fingers, chest, and stomach from an unidentified explosive device. Seventeen policemen received medical treatment; the most serious case was Zoran Danilovic, who had been hit in the head by a rock.

Two people were dead on arrival at the emergency center. Jasmina "Minka" Jovanovic was run over by a truck in Kneza Milosa Street. Momcilo Stakic died of a heart attack in front of the Federal Parliament.

At 6.00 P.M., the police headquarters at 29th November Street went off the air.

TWENTY-TWO

THE LAST POLICE STATION

At 6 P.M. on October 5, the government of Yugoslavia changed hands. Milosevic had been toppled in just two and a half hours. The establishment of a new government had begun. Part of rebel Belgrade was celebrating. Another part was still fighting the old government—not its remnants but the symbols of its power.

Democratic Opposition of Serbia, the winner, wasn't doing anything yet. Some DOS members were in the streets, others in Covic's heavily guarded headquarters, listening to the echoes of the ongoing skirmishes in the city.

The new government was mostly created by the disintegration of the old. The terrified establishment had simply fled. There was no government, no police, no state media, no ruling party. Slobodan Cerovic, giving his account for this book, says it was obvious that the system had been overturned. "Basically the government no longer existed. The only issue now was when this would be legally sorted out. Nothing else."

Everything that embodied the state and the regime had been in confusion. Now it all fell into the hands of a surprised DOS. People who until a couple of hours earlier had been bent on destroying things now had to turn to building something. It was for this reason that Vojislav Kostunica visited the Patriarchate, the head office of the Serbian Orthodox Church. He emerged from that imposing building accompanied by Bishop Atanasije Rakita, who would stay with DOS throughout the night. The new government had the blessing of the church. Now it had to deal with worldly matters. There were two grave dangers in Belgrade.

First of all, the city was in flames.

The sky to the southeast was already black with smoke from the RTS and the Parliament buildings. When the fire brigade said, "Let's go!" the firefighters were in the garage in 35 seconds.

"I wasn't comfortable about it," one burly fireman said later. "We had been watching TV Pancevo in the club and had seen the police coming out of the television [building] with their hands in the air. And now we had to go there. It didn't feel good, I have to tell you!"

Six engines set out from the base. At the corner of Cvijiceva and Takovska Streets they came to a halt. Garbage containers blocked the road ahead and more appeared behind, blocking their retreat. "Don't block us, people," the commander of the fire brigade shouted, "we're only going to put the fire out!" But the mob hurled rocks at them from behind the dumpsters.

"Keep your helmet on and watch out for glass," one fireman said. "That was all we could do."

In the end the mob let them go; all they could do was return to their base. Men in uniform weren't welcome in Takovska Street that afternoon.

Back at the base they heard the DOS appeal, again on TV Pancevo. They were calling on firefighters to come to the center and appealing to the people to let them through. "Let's go," the commander ordered again. Somehow they managed to get through to the RTS building, now a blazing beacon in the center of the city. The fire was melting glass, rubber, and plastic. Windows were cracking from the heat. Huge fireballs were crashing from the upper floors. "Okay," said the commander. "Roll them out." They started hauling the hoses out of the trucks. He sent two men into the building. They searched the whole building, bowed against the heat and wearing masks. On the less smoky floors there were kids no older than 14 running everywhere, filching everything left in the building: cables, fax machines, telephones, and so on. "Like locusts," the fireman thought. Some guys with baseball bats also ran past. They asked for his helmet. "Are you crazy?" he replied. Smoke was pouring in from the Aberdareva Street building.

They went up to the fourth floor. Nobody was there. The temperature in that part of the building was more than 700° Fahrenheit, and their extinguishers began to boil. When they went out to replace them, they were redeployed on the hoses. The fire had to be contained.

The blaze in the RTS building was worst in the narrow section facing the street. It was burning from the top down, and the steel and timber structure was caving in. The fire then began to spread from the basement up, through the interior of the building. The firemen tried to cut it off at the second floor, in the stairwells. Then they ran out of water.

"The Belgrade hydrants," a fireman said later, "were all in a terrible state. We usually take water from the Danube: we take the tankers there and pump it in. But now we couldn't get down to the Danube. I found a low-pressure hydrant inside the building and put out as much of the fire as I could until the cistern began boiling again. When I went out into the street I could see fire breaking out again at the top of the building. And then came our two tankers, with ten tons of water each."

It took more than two hours to put out the fire on Takovska Street. During that time one fireman used up three sets of breathing gear. Each lasts 40 minutes. He was already drenched with sweat when he changed the first one. After the third he was sent back to the base.

The fire station was full of police. There were far fewer of those from Vranje, Leskovac, and Pirot than had arrived that morning. They were sitting in the mess hall, beaten, stripped of their weapons and uniforms.

The fireman had time only for a shower before he was sent as reinforcement to the Parliament building. First they put out the fire in the basement, facing the park in Vlajkoviceva Street. When they came out they were told that there were flames leaping from four windows on Takovska Street. "Where did that come from?" asked the fireman. He'd seen no fire on that side when he arrived. The informant only shrugged.

Now the side of the building facing Takovska Street was ablaze. The fireman poured five tons of water through the windows from the water cannon. "It was like spitting on it," he said later. "No effect at all!"

Another tanker arrived to help. They managed to stop the fire with the twin jets of water. Then they went inside, crawling. The temperature was more than 1, 800 degrees. When they finally emerged they were told that the Vlajkoviceva Street side had burst into flames again. "What can you do?" said the fireman, giving his account for this book. "You change your gear, and it speeds your metabolism up by a factor of four. In you go again and put the fire out. I thought that it was finally over."

Then he saw them. They were running from Palmoticeva Street, five or six kids, holding bottles with burning rags sticking out of them. "Hey!" he shouted. "Don't do that!" The Takovska Street side of the building burst into flames again.

The firemen were ready to give up. "You'd better make up your minds whether you want it to burn or not," they told the DOS security guards lined up around the building.

The firefighters finally secured access from Palmoticeva Street. The fire in the Parliament wasn't out until 9:30 A.M. on October 6. By then, everything else in Belgrade was long over, including the affairs on Majke Jevrosime Street and Student Square.

"Collateral damage." That's the modern euphemism for misfortunes of the sort that befell the Majke Jevrosime Street police station and the Socialist Party of Serbia headquarters in Student Square during and after the battles for the Parliament and RTS. They were destroyed. It hadn't been planned.

The location of the police station was unfortunate, which is nothing new in the history of wars and revolutions. Pera, then a Genoese colony on the Golden Horn, was separated from Constantinople only by a narrow stretch of water when Mehmed II conquered the city in six weeks, from April 6 to May 28, in 1453.

On October 5, 2000, only two streets separated the police station from the Parliament and RTS. One to the south, another to the west.

There was one difference between the two battles that was of decisive significance. The people of Pera didn't interfere much in the defense of the last bastion of Byzantium. The Stari Grad police, however, kitted themselves up with batons, flak jackets, helmets, and shields and ran out into Vlajkoviceva Street at 3:45 P.M. to defend the symbol of Milosevic's state. Some suffered broken fingers and arms and a head or two was cracked. They retreated to the station, tails between their legs. Then, from 4 P.M. to 6 P.M. without rhyme or reason, they launched a hail of tear-gas cartridges from the roof of the building, scattering them all over the area around the Parliament and RTS.

That tipped the scales. Mehmed II, having conquered Constantinople, taxed the people of Pera but otherwise left them in peace. Belgrade's revolutionaries, on October 5, 2000, having seized the Parliament, charged in a fury on the police station.

This was when Velja Ilic lost his water tanker. He had brought it from Cacak because he believed the siege would last much longer. The demonstrators would need water to drink, he thought, and he ordered a water tanker to be included in the long convoy. Unluckily for the tanker, it was parked too close to Majke Jevrosime Street.

When the battle began in the narrow, smoke-filled street, one revolutionary jumped into the tanker, started it up and crashed it several times into the front wall of the police station. The entrance was narrow, and the tanker couldn't fit through. The wall around the doorway was smashed to pieces. According to a police report the tanker assault happened at 5:50 P.M. This is one of the few pieces of information on the chronology of the events in and around the police station. Everyone was far too engrossed in the situation at the Parliament and, later, RTS to keep track of what was happening on this secondary battlefield. Even police headquarters wasn't concerned. The Stari Grad commander, Branko Stojadinovic, reported twice to Avala 10. At 5:10 P.M. he told them, "They're in front of the station. They pushed us back!"

Avala 10: "Roger. Wait!"

Twenty minutes later it was even worse.

Stojadinovic to Avala 10: "The situation is serious."

Avala 10: "Do you have any force?"

Stojadinovic: "Not much."

Avala 10: "Wait!"

Headquarters was more concerned about the demonstrators in front of the Aberdareva Street entrance of RTS. Nobody had time to worry about Stari Grad.

Nobody knows exactly when the station fell; it wasn't recorded on the police radio band. It's assumed that the fall occurred after radio communication ceased and the police headquarters on 29th November Street effectively ceased to exist. The story in police circles was that it happened at 7:45, but it's unlikely that Stojadinovic and his men could have held out for two hours and thirty five minutes after the dramatic call at 5:10 P.M. telling Avala 10 that the demonstrators were in front of the station.

Press photographs published over the next few days also indicate that the Stari Grad police had laid down their arms much earlier. The pictures showing policemen leaving the station with their hands raised were taken in daylight. At 7:45 P.M. in October, the sun has long set on Belgrade.

The photographs give rise to another suspicion. Daylight is pretty much gone by 6:00 P.M. in Belgrade in October. Is it possible that the station fell while the headquarters was still operating and that none of the police chiefs even noticed?

Ceda Jovanovic isn't sure about the time, but he is certain that he went straight to the police station after leaving the Parliament. Police were firing tear gas from the roof. There were cars and garbage containers overturned in the street. He found more than five hundred people in front of the station. In the police reports they are referred to as "kids, Red Star fans and people with criminal records."

All Ceda saw was that their eyes were red and they were ready to tear someone apart. A few policemen in grimy uniforms, unarmed, were standing in front of the building attempting to negotiate. Behind them, in the station itself, there were more police lined up, scowling and clutching their automatic weapons. Behind the broken windows, one smiling policeman pointed to a Serbian flag and raised three fingers.

"Maybe you can help us," said one of the police negotiators. Ceda Jovanovic's face is well known in Belgrade. The policeman addressed him as "Mr. Ceda," and took him to talk to Stari Grad commander Branko Stojadinovic. He was sitting in his office, which had long been full of tear gas. His eyes were brimming. Ceda recognized him as the man who only a week before had stopped DOS from setting up a platform for a rally.

Time to settle accounts. He offered the commander a chance to surrender and observed that if he'd let the people have some fun a week earlier, probably nothing would have happened. It wasn't true, of course, but what revolutionary cares about details like that? Particularly when there's a chance for a little payback.

Stojadinovic proposed that he stay inside and the demonstrators stay outside, leaving things the way they were. Jovanovic refused. The circumstances were on his side. As they spoke, a hail of rocks landed on the station. The mob pushed the police aside and rushed in. Fists were flying. The negotiations were over. "We managed to get our people to go out," said Jovanovic. They lined up outside and the policemen emerged, one by one, to run the gauntlet. Then the station burst into flames.

Slobodan Pajic, the former police officer who rescued his old colleagues from the Kosovska Street lobby of the Parliament, saw the Stari Grad police station incident as one of the most disgraceful episodes in police history. "The Stari Grad station building could be defended by one man with a single rifle, if need be," said Pajic. The way he saw it, a police commander could even do it single-handedly, but only if he had already refused to intervene on the streets of Belgrade. Majke Jevrosime Street is narrow, the entrance is in an alley; in short, the conditions are almost ideal for a simple defense. It seems it just wasn't Branko Stojadinovic's day on October 5. On that day he made every mistake in the book.

The destruction of the Socialist Party of Serbia headquarters in Student Square happened in quite different circumstances. The premises are at the other side of downtown, separated from the Parliament and RTS by a number of long blocks and broad squares, quite removed from the battle going on. Neither the cries of the demonstrators nor the tear gas could reach the Socialist headquarters.

It was basically a victim of the post-revolution party. The demonstrators rushed on the Socialist offices that evening, when the celebrations were already under way in Belgrade's streets.

The Socialist Party building was also the victim of an oversight by the DOS organizers. Djindjic, Covic, and the rest of them feared that after the Parliament and RTS, the people might turn on the Serbian Presidency, across Pioneer Park from the Federal Parliament and adjacent to the City Assembly, to which the DOS headquarters had moved at 6:00 P.M. They were also concerned that the Serbian Parliament, directly across Srpskih Vladara Street from the presidency, could be attacked. Another possible target they considered was the Serbian Government building in Nemanjina Street, through which the angry people of Cacak had driven to the Parliament that morning. DOS had all these buildings under heavy guard. The only damage any of them suffered was one broken window at the Serbian Parliament and one at the Serbian Presidency, separated from the battlefield only by Pioneer Park, which was packed with demonstrators.

DOS leaders simply overlooked the Socialist headquarters.

Unfortunately, so had the police. About ten officers from the river police had been ordered into the building that morning. Their home station, not far from the confluence of the Sava and the Danube, was the closest to Student Square. When police headquarters stopped working and police communications went off the air, the ten officers were forgotten about. Nobody told them what was going on. Left completely without information, the poor wretches stayed in the Socialist Party building.

The regime didn't take care of its people at all. Branislav Ivkovic, minister for culture in the Serbian government and the president of the Vracar branch of the party, had no one to call when the branch premises in Kursulina Street were demolished. The nearby office of the Foundation to Fight Alcoholism, AIDS, and Drug Addiction, established by the Socialists, was also destroyed. Ivkovic gave his account: "Late that evening, four young men in a white Renault 4 pulled up outside my house in Molerova Street, tore the gate apart and came to my door."

"I thought about shooting," said Ivkovic. He didn't manage to contact the police until the next morning and had no communication whatsoever with either the government or the leadership of the party. He learned about the arrival of the convoys in Belgrade at 2 P.M. It irritated him to hear it from CNN and Radio Indeks.

"I rang the Government Information Center to tell them where I was, hoping that somebody would call me. Nobody did." He added that the Serbian government hadn't even met on October 4, the eve of the planned rally. Obviously the chaos had begun long before October 5.

The only contact Ivkovic had with the authorities on D-day was with the City Committee of the Socialist Party, which was also in the building on Student Square. "I was in touch with them until 8 P.M. After that they, too, came under attack."

The Socialist Party building was broken into at about 11 P.M. The boisterous mob, eager to destroy and plunder the symbols of Milosevic's power, tried three times to break down the heavy metal door. The vice president of the City Committee, Milutin Djordjevic, managed to heave a large metal safe against the door. Finally demonstrators arrived with crowbars. The door twisted and cracked. The safe was shoved aside. Djordjevic fled through a rear exit.

The mob ran into the confused and frightened police officers. The police had no desire to defend the symbols of power and fled to the restaurant in the basement. About 70 demonstrators, armed and angry, waited in ambush at the top of the stairs. The smell of blood was in the air. A priest from the nearby offices of the archdiocese of Raska and Prizren tried to calm the mob down. "Brothers . . ." he began.

"Cut the bullshit, Father," said one of the demonstrators, and they threw him out of the building.

At about 11:30 P.M., one terrified policeman, his face white as a sheet, rushed into the office of Vladan Batic's Democratic Christian Party in Zmaja on Nocaja Street, a hundred or so yards away. "Help!" he shouted from the doorway.

At the same time, the telephone rang at the Democratic Alternative offices. Pajic was told that more police had been found. They were in the Socialist Party building in Student Square. There had been gunfire. It was a serious conflict. He set off without a word.

Batic had only just entered his party office. "It's a madhouse right across the city," he said cheerfully. At that moment, somebody shouted "Help!" from behind him. "What now?" thought Batic, and turned around. A man in uniform, pale and frightened, was waving one of his party's business cards. "They'll kill us all," he wailed. "Please!"

Pajic and Batic met at the entrance of the Socialist Party building. The last remaining windows were shattering around him. "It was a cataclysm," Batic said later. Everything inside the building was smashed. They walked across the broken glass, watching people dragging their loot down the stairs. Their eyes stung with tear gas. The mob greeted Batic with a victorious cheer. He waved, smiled, and went down to the basement.

The police were huddled in the last room. The rest of the basement was full of revolutionaries. "Dogs!" they were shouting. "You fucking sons of bitches! Dogs! We're going to kill you!"

By the time the DOS leaders arrived, the police were shaking with fear. "I'll walk in front of you," promised Batic. "No one's going to touch you." Pajic brought up the rear of this odd procession. The priest reappeared out of nowhere. At the top of the stairs they stopped. The front line was waiting for them with snarling faces and clubs raised.

Vladan Batic decided it was time to make a speech. So he began. He spoke of Milosevic's hostages, about the families of the police among the demonstrators, about the victims of a madman, about the need to have police, about Serbs, about democracy. Finally he lost patience. "What do you want?" he cried. "You want to shoot them here and now?"

The mob parted. "You're a prick, man!" said one of the demonstrators, the ringleader, and left the building. The procession moved slowly off toward the exit. The demonstrators left the officers alone, trying only to grab their weapons as they passed. Pajic slapped their hands away.

Back at Batic's headquarters, they sat down to a glass of slivovitz. The Socialist Party building was left to the mob.

The mob that day also trashed the City Committee of the Yugoslav Left, on the corner of Kneza Milosa and Proleterskih Brigada Streets, and the Palilula branch of the Socialist Party. But the most thorough demolition job of all was done on an exclusive perfume shop in Terazije Square owned by Milosevic's son, Marko.

TWENTY-THREE

POLITIKA FALLS TO DOS

Captain Dragan, looking out of his apartment window, saw smoke gushing from the Parliament. He said his prayers, pulled on the trousers of his uniform, fastened his Scorpion machine pistol into its holster, put a leather jacket on over it, and set off. One of DOS's most important plans was about to swing into action.

At the beginning of the twenty-first century, the media are the key to politics, war, and revolution. The victory now looming on the horizon had to be secured. The safest way to do that was to proclaim that it has already happened. Proclamations are the business of the media. It was Captain Dragan's job to seize Studio B.

In the DOS scenario, Milosevic's political death had to happen in the same virtual reality as his political life. For years his newspapers, his radio stations, and most of all his television had reinvented reality, rearranging it, painting and varnishing it, and serving it up to the people of Serbia. For a long time, average Serbs had no idea that Serbia was at war or that it had lost those senseless wars. The number of casualties, either on the Serbian side or on the other sides, has never been published. After the debacle in Kosovo, the last of the series, the engineers of reality created the "heroes of the victory." Milosevic, loathed and shunned, expelled from all European and global organizations, received the ambassadors of non-existent states. In Virtual Serbia, he was a mighty statesman, a tireless fighter for freedom and independence.

Democratic Opposition of Serbia had prepared a treat for him: the takeover of Studio B, the interception of the RTS frequencies, and an announcement of his defeat well before it actually happened. Milosevic, DOS thought, had to be defeated on the grounds he had long claimed for himself—the prime-time evening television news—before a virtual crowd of 3.5 million households.

But on October 5, fact happened faster than fiction, as it had many times before. Milosevic's defeat came suddenly. The whole system fell, Milosevic with it, in a domino effect, before anyone could announce anything.

The throne on which the regime sat was already rotten. When the first leg was kicked away, everything crashed to the ground.

Captain Dragan still didn't know about it. The two thousand angry people outside Beogradjanka, where Studio B was located, didn't know it yet either. They each had their own revolutionary assignment and were concentrating only on that. They were thinking about the seventy five policemen on the fifth floor of the tallest building in central Belgrade who, by the revolutionary rules of the day, had to be thrown out and thrashed. The police themselves were the only ones who had any inkling that it might all be over. But they didn't know what to do either about this knowledge or the mob of angry people outside waiting for them.

Captain Dragan set out to negotiate.

The Studio B staff, the ones who were aware of the DOS plans, had already tried. When the first attempt failed, it was Dragan's turn. If he didn't succeed, the men he'd smuggled into the building the night before would swing into action. Armed and ready, they were in position at every entrance to the fifth floor and were waiting for his signal. He was curt with the police: "You can cooperate with me or wait here for the mob to come up. There are already police dead in Majke Jevrosime Street." Lies were fair game in revolutions, he told himself. Especially when it came to seizing the regime's lying media. That was all the justification he needed.

The policemen stared.

"Dead!" repeated Dragan.

Somebody sent word that five thousand more people had arrived in the past few minutes. One of the police mentioned headquarters. "There's no headquarters anymore," Dragan told him. He was convincing enough. The police laid down their arms.

The man who had seized Studio B was experienced enough to keep everything under control. The policemen put their weapons in bags prepared for them. A number of them were in civilian clothes. They left the building first, with the weapons. The rest of the police, escorted and protected by

Dragan's men, passed unharmed through the mob. He led them personally to the corner of Nemanjina and Kneza Milosa Streets. There they were met by soldiers from the barracks attached to the old General Staff building in Kneza Milosa Street that had been destroyed by the NATO bombing.

At 6 P.M. the liberated Studio B was back on the air.

Everything else fell one by one. Milosevic's mighty media empire fell, channel by channel, newsroom by newsroom, straight into the hands of DOS. Politika was first.

For Zarko Korac of the Social Democratic Union, it was shock upon shock. They stopped him in the street again. He left No. 3 Terazije Street and made for his party headquarters, Belgrade's streets were abuzz with celebration. Somebody grabbed his sleeve.

"There's nobody at Politika," a young man said. He hung on to Korac's arm, his words heavy with intent. "I'm a cameraman," he explained to the surprised academic. "We want to broadcast a program. Will you come?"

None of the DOS leaders, the president of the Social Democratic Union included, had imagined that Politika would fall. When they'd discussed media at DOS, nobody had even mentioned the company. The opposition leaders had been preoccupied with Radio Television Serbia.

"I'll come," Korac said straightaway. He had realized what was happening when the police had sought him out to surrender to. He had become a figure of authority. As soon as someone becomes the sought instead of the seeker, they know they're in power. It didn't matter that no one had expected this to happen. Nor did it matter that the word of the DOS victory had spread through the city while Djindjic and Covic still didn't know whether they could leave the office in Terazije Square without being arrested or killed. All that mattered was that those institutions on which Milosevic had depended now believed that DOS had the upper hand. They began believing it when he stopped protecting them. When the police walked out of those institutions on October 5, Milosevic went with them.

Politika, the oldest media company in Serbia, was one of them. Two police squads had left the building at 6 P.M. through the rear exit on 29th November Street. Since then there'd been virtually nobody in the building. Korac and the young cameraman set off for the tall Politika building on Makedonska Street. Belgrade parted to let them through.

The fall of TV Bastille was the last of the ugly scenes on Belgrade's streets. The rest of the events were much less dramatic, or at least they appeared to be so. This applied particularly to the occupation of Milosevic's remaining fortresses. At Politika, for instance, the old guard's resistance amounted to cutting the power to the elevators. So Zarko Korac had to climb 17 floors to the company's television studio.

"It was like the aftermath of nuclear war," Korac said later. "Everything was deserted. Totally."

He was the first guest on the new TV Politika. He sat down next to the young anchor. She was wearing a badge that read "I'm Kostunica, too."

The new Politika program began at 7:30 P.M. with the statement, "Politika is a liberated national company."

Just three hours earlier the old editorial staff had presented news about the activities of now former Prime Minister Momir Bulatovic's government and of conflict between the Palestinians and the Israelis.

Now there were hundreds of people outside the building watching Zarko Korac on television sets behind the plate glass facade of Politika's imposing lobby. A placard proclaiming "This is ours, now!" was enough to spare the largest company in the old regime's media empire.

Ceda Jovanovic of the Democratic Party ran into Politika just a few minutes after Korac. He went straight to the fifth floor, into the newsroom of the daily *Politika* newspaper, saw Korac on a television set, and sat down.

"I was in complete shock," he said later. "Since I'd rushed out of Covic's party office, I'd run into a brawl, then to the Parliament, then to the police station, and finally to Politika. I had no idea what was happening. I came to the newsroom, and they asked me for a statement. They asked me what was going on. How would I know what was happening? I just told them that I was delighted. Just that."

Jovanovic still hadn't got himself together when Covic called.

"What's with Radio Belgrade?" Covic, the Democratic Alternative leader, asked.

"What's with Radio Belgrade?" repeated Jovanovic, puzzled. Then he realized.

He hung up, said, "See you later" to the people in the newsroom, and ran. Radio Belgrade was only 50 yards away from Politika. And the building was in darkness.

"Open up!" shouted Jovanovic, and banged on the big front door of Radio Belgrade. "Open up or I'll break the door down," he was roaring when someone from the darkness on the other side of the door said, "Come around to the rear entrance."

They entered the huge, dark building from Hilandarska Street. Ceda's guys had their pistols cocked. "You're not going to do anything to me, are you?" asked the man who let them in.

They groped through the dark until they found someone who knew how to turn the lights on. That person was also worried what they would do to him.

Jovanovic had already lost count of which floor they were on when they found a journalist, Milan Spicek, who showed them to the radio control room. Ceda went into the studio. "You're on the air," they told him from the control room.

"I still didn't have any idea what had happened," he said, "whether the police would come back, whether they would recapture what we had already seized. I knew nothing."

"My congratulations to everyone," he said on air. "What's happened today is wonderful."

One of the guys told him to shut up. "If they hear that we've taken over Radio Belgrade they'll send someone here to blast us straight away."

"You're listening to the liberated Radio Belgrade," Jovanovic finished. He instructed Spicek and the control room to play music and shout "Freedom!" between the tracks. On the way out of the building he ran into Vladan Batic. Upstairs, the radio resumed transmission.

At the DOS office they were counting the remaining media companies. TV Pink, Borba, Vecernje novosti, Tanjug, all the ones they hadn't even thought about before October 5. The power that had fallen from the sky and was now running through the Belgrade Streets had to be harnessed. They assigned Tanjug, the state news agency, to G17's Predrag Markovic.

The large, curved building in Obilicev Crescent, a fine example of socialist-realism architecture, was also in darkness when Markovic reached it. But it wasn't completely empty.

"Who are you?" the security guard asked.

"Markovic. G17 Plus," he replied.

"They're waiting for you," said the guard.

A woman led the puzzled Markovic through the corridors to an office. The man sitting behind the desk politely introduced himself. "I'm Micic, the former acting director."

Markovic realized that October 5 must have been a nightmare for the man. "You're free," he said, "you may go home."

Micic seemed almost cheerful as he left.

The new Tanjug began operating.

Meanwhile, Mladjan Dinkic had made a guest appearance on TV Pink, the entertainment channel owned by Zeljko Mitrovic, a board member of the Yugoslav Left. Manojlo Vukotic went to Borba. On his way upstairs in the building on Nikola Pasic Square he also took over another regime daily, *Vecernje Novosti*, which was housed in the same building. A young man entered from the rear entrance in Kosovska Street at the same time.

Darko, the young man, didn't exactly believe in the revolution. He hadn't even taken part in it, convinced that nothing would come of it. Only once it had happened, once the city was on fire, did he begin to believe. Then he set out for the building of *Dnevni Telegraf*, the newspaper destroyed by Milosevic. Its owner, journalist Slavko Curuvija, had been gunned down at the front door of his home on April 11, 1999. Darko had been working there when the police barged into *Dnevni Telegraf* in October 1998. They trashed the fifth floor of the Borba building before leaving. This was punishment, the first punishment, for what Curuvija had written about Milosevic and his regime in his two publications, the daily *Dnevni Telegraf* and the fortnightly *Evropljanin*.

The police had removed all the equipment, even the office furniture. More than a hundred people, Darko included, soon lost their jobs as a result. Curuvija lost his life, hit from behind by 17 bullets.

"I just wanted to go upstairs," Darko said later, "to see who was using our offices and throw them out of the fifth floor. That was all."

He got a team together. The security guards at the Kosovska Street entrance didn't even try to stop them. The fifth floor was empty. "Just as well," thought Darko. On their way out of the building his guys roughed up the security guards. The men who, since October 1998, hadn't allowed anyone from *Dnevni Telegraf* to enter the building were handed a few solid punches.

TWENTY-FOUR

THE NEW RADIO TELEVISION SERBIA

Ivica Stojkovic had prayed that morning in front of the icon, an oil lamp burning below it. He was afraid, and his fear lent the city an eerie look as he set out for Kosutnjak. Empty and quiet, no one on the streets, no police, the city looked vast and ready to engulf everybody. Ivica Stojkovic had good reason to be afraid: It was his task on October 5 to do something nobody had ever done before, to black out every television screen in Serbia by cutting off the RTS transmission.

The most important moment of the entire day, the beginning of revolutionary broadcasts on the state television network, came as a shock to the whole nation. As with most momentous events, it happened suddenly and took everyone by surprise.

Petar Lazovic, one of the people who seized control of the whole RTS network on the evening of October 5, says that it wasn't until days later that he realized what he had done. "It was a classic delayed reaction. I went to bed and then suddenly thought, 'My God, what if they'd come back?' It was only then that the panic hit me."

Seven people, most of them former employees, took over the leadership of the country's most powerful media. Petar Lazovic, Nenad Ristic, Gordana Susa, Miodrag Zupanc, Vladimir Arsic, Jovan Valcic, and Mihailo Ristic sat around a table and signed their names on a sheet of ruled paper. Nebojsa Covic signed and dated the document. That was how it ended.

It had begun on stage.

The Dusko Radovic theater was crowded with technicians, cameramen, editors, journalists, directors, sound technicians. The tiny auditorium of the theater looked like an overstocked shop with RTS staff bulging out of every entrance. Strike Committee member Milena Vucetic had just returned from a meeting at the Independence Union. She jumped up to the stage and the theater fell quiet. "Are you sure?" she asked. "Shall we black them out?"

Miodrag Zupanc held his breath. Milena Vucetic took out her cell phone and began dialing.

"Turn it off!" they cried.

"Turn it off!" Milena said into her cell.

Zupanc breathed again.

"We're going to turn it off," the guys from the program control room told Ivica Stojkovic that morning when he arrived at work. "That's the proposal, they still have to pass it." Ivica felt his palms sweating. There were a lot of people in the control room. Ivica, Buda Pekovic, and Bane Simic with a rattle and an Otpor sticker. The nerve center of any television station is the room from which the transmission signal is switched on or off. The RTS control room is seven and a half miles away from Takovska Street, behind a heavy steel door. Nine years earlier, during the demonstrations of March 9, 1991, it was guarded by police with Kalashnikovs. The RTS building in Kosutnjak was more or less empty now. There were a few people in the magnetoscope division, the room from which broadcast tapes are played, two or three unarmed security guards and these three in the program control room. No one else. Ivica checked outside the door from time to time anyway.

"The big question was how it should be done," he said later. "If we just black it out suddenly and some woman from, I don't know, let's say Arilje, has children in Belgrade at the demonstrations and sees the television suddenly cut out, what will she think? She'll collapse!"

"'We should broadcast the news and something else for five or six minutes,' someone suggested, 'and when it's finished just not broadcast anything else. That would do.'"

Gordana Manevic, in charge of tapes in the magnetoscope division, agreed. Now they only had to wait for the decision of the Strike Committee. Time had never passed so slowly for Ivica. Sometime before 2 P.M. Radisa Petrovic called. "It looks as though we're going to turn it off," he said after he hung up. "Milena will let Goca know as soon as the committee decides."

The studio in Takovska Street called program control.

Staka Novovic was standing by to present the 2 P.M. news.

"Ready?" asked the people in Takovska Street.

"Ready," said Ivica.

"I wanted to tell them 'ready for the last time,' but I didn't dare," he said later.

He pushed the button. The serious face of Staka Novovic was reproduced on television screens throughout Serbia.

Then, in Gordana Manevic's office, the telephone rang.

"Turn it off!" said Milena Vucetic, seven and a half miles away.

"Turn it off!" repeated Gordana Manevic to the people in program control. Ivica just stood up.

Five minutes later, television screens throughout Serbia were blacked out.

Nenad Ristic wasn't aware of all these developments. He had taken a lot of tear gas in front of the Parliament, he had a pain in the right half of his head as though someone had hammered a nail into it, and now, on top of everything, he was lost. He was alone, on his hands and knees somewhere in Terazije Square, vomiting. He has no idea how long it was before he met his colleagues again near the Russian Czar restaurant in Knez Mihailova Street. Then the tear gas began to spread there from who knows where. "Home," said Ristic, and got into the car. He tuned in to Radio Indeks. "There are curtains on fire in the television building." He felt nauseated again.

The tear gas caught up with Radisa Petrovic near the Lasta bus station. That was when he realized he'd parked in the wrong place. Revolutionary Belgrade on October 5 was using anything with four wheels for both defense and attack. Radisa thought it would be a good idea to move his car. He set out for home. The fire he left behind in the city center wasn't his concern. He had quit the television and was certain he'd never have anything to do with it again. "Home," he was thinking. New Belgrade, thank God, wasn't far away that day. Red-eyed and still choking, he called from the door for a brandy. He was on his second when the telephone rang. It was Milena Vucetic. "We're going to Kosutnjak. We're starting up the television."

Rade Veljanovski thought the people in the Media Center didn't look excited enough about the change that had just taken place. So he ran down to Independence. Most of the RTS Strike Committee was already there: Bojan Bosiljcic, Zupanc, Radovan Pantovic, Dragan Mikovic. "I asked them whether there was somewhere from which we could broadcast a television program," said Veljanovski. It was impossible in either Aberdareva Street or Takovska Street. Somebody remembered Kosutnjak. "Is there anyone there?" asked Veljanovski. Nebojsa Covic put the same question to Veljanovski later on, when DOS also got involved in the scheme.

"Police?"

"None," replied Veljanovski. "We checked."

Petar Lazovic nearly died when he saw police, armed to the teeth, running into the RTS building in Kosutnjak. "We're with you!" the man leading them cried out when he saw Lazovic's face. "We're here to protect you."

"My God," thought Lazovic, "even the police have crossed over!"

It had all happened just a few hours before.

Far away from the celebration in the streets of Belgrade the creation of a revolutionary army began. At first it was only an idea in the minds of a few people, to defend what they called "the will of the people." It needed to be strong enough to defend that will against any attempt at a counterattack by the regime. Two days later this army included special police forces, the Police Brigade, the Special Operations unit, and the anti-terrorist unit. They were to be coordinated by General Vlastimir Djordjevic. Actual command would rest with DOS.

On the evening of October 5, the only guarantee DOS had was the word of Milorad "Legija" Ulemek. There was something else on their side, although the leaders weren't aware of it yet. In an apartment at 43 Kosovska Street, Colonel Bosko Buha smoked five cigarettes. The first in his life. Later that evening he left the apartment in a sweatsuit. When he got home, his 13-year-old son asked him, "What happened, Dad?"

His father's explanation was hard to believe. "You know, it's as though you were a Red Star fan all your life and then suddenly you realise that's a mistake and you start following Partizan."

His son didn't believe a word of it. But that was exactly how Buha felt.

"How could I explain?" he said later. "I had lived in one system for 40 years: Tito's Pioneers, Tito's youth, Tito's communists. I just went on in the same way after that and then, suddenly, someone slapped me hard. I came to my senses and said, 'Hang on, fuck you!' That's how I felt!"

The moment that had brought Buha to his senses was when Covic came to the rescue of the trapped police. That and the report from his deputy, Vladimir Ilic, when he managed to reach police headquarters at 29th November Street with most of the brigade. "Ilic went into headquarters," Buha said later, "and asked for them to put a stop to the action. He explained that I was up here, under siege, that there were a lot more police out there, that we were hostages, and that the action should be called off to save us. They didn't even look at him. They were watching television! He left and led the brigade back to our base."

It all fell into place. When Buha, still in his sweatsuit, reached the huge barracks on Trebevicka Street in Banovo Brdo that is the home of the powerful Belgrade Police Brigade, the decisions had already been made. His officers shared his opinion. As far as they were concerned, the Ministry of Internal Affairs no longer existed.

Luck was on Buha's side from that point on. First, the location. The brigade is miles away from both the 29th November police headquarters and the central headquarters of the Belgrade police as well as the ministry in Kneza Milosa Street. Anyone who wanted to contact Buha had to come to him. If anyone telephoned from police headquarters, the duty officer at the brigade would reply "The colonel isn't here." Moreover, the first thing Buha did when he got to Banovo Brdo was deploy well-armed men on all the access roads to the barracks.

The chaos in the Ministry of Internal Affairs seemed to support the police colonel's plans. The generals were more or less fed up, and the city's central police headquarters were surrounded. Branko Djuric, the chief of the City Secretariat for Internal Affairs, received a DOS delegation to hear their ultimatum. "He was under a kind of house arrest," Zoran Djindjic said later. That meant he had no time to deal with the rebel brigade.

And finally it was Covic who got to Buha first. He said he had come to ask a favor. He asked Buha bluntly to come over to the DOS side and secure the television building in Kosutnjak.

Chief of Staff General Nebojsa Pavkovic later claimed that the reason the troops of the Seventy-Second Brigade had been in Kosutnjak on the evening of October 5 was to secure Zastava Film. "Our film library is there," said Pavkovic. "The archives are fairly significant and I sent part of the Seventy-Second, a squad, that's about ten men, to secure the facility. We didn't even know that the television studio at Kosutnjak was operating."

The Seventy-Second Brigade is an elite unit of the Yugoslav Army consisting of military specialists. Zastava Film is in Kosutnjak, less than six-tenths of a mile away from Radio Television Serbia. Perhaps there's nothing unusual in facilities such as a military archive and film library being guarded on days such as October 5 by a crack army unit rather than ordinary military police.

What does seem odd is that Nebojsa Covic ran into the Seventy-Second Brigade when he arrived at Kosutnjak. Sometime later, at Zastava Film, he met the commander of this "squad of about ten men," an officer of the rank of colonel. Pavkovic identified the commander for this book as Colonel Milovanovic.

Colonels customarily command larger units than squads, but Covic wasn't concerned about that at the moment. His men were around Zastava Film and there were military specialists around Zastava Film as well. This battle which had not yet begun was still to be joined by Buha and possibly another squad of the Seventy-Second.

The negotiations went on for an hour and a half, according to Covic. He and Colonel Milovanovic finally arrived at an agreement of non-aggression. "Covic was told that everything would be normal," said Pavkovic, describing the agreement.

The people who were setting up the new television program knew nothing about the negotiations at Zastava Film. Nor did they have any idea that they would have police security later that night.

Just to be on the safe side, the Independence Union sent about 20 metal workers, armed only with crowbars. Covic also sent his 20 guys. Petar Lazovic, giving his account for this book, described them as being armed "like an aircraft carrier." And that was just the beginning.

Nenad Ristic was still at home, his whole body numb with tiredness. "Call your colleagues," his wife kept saying. "Call them," she repeated until he could stand it no more. He dialed. "Come to Kosutnjak," they said.

Radisa Petrovic was already there. Zupanc, too. Bojan Bosiljcic and Milena Vucetic were there as well. Petar Lazovic took his heart pills first and then came over. Ivica Stojkovic took some tranquilizers and then he too set out. They were shocked to find the Kosutnjak studio in total disorder. The keys to the program control room weren't there. Some regime loyalist had been there after Ivica and the others had left. When they finally opened the television network's electronic nerve center with spare keys used in case of fire they found chaos. The cables had been switched around.

"It took us two and a half hours to start transmitting," Radisa Petrovic said later. "I shall never forget finally seeing the return signal from Avala."

Bojan Bosiljcic came into the studio.

"Ready?" asked the director.

"Ready," replied program control.

"Dear viewers," Bosiljcic began in classic RTS style.

"Fuck that!" cried Zoran Djindjic and jumped to his feet. "Victory! Victory!" he shouted. In addition to the DOS leaders, the ambassadors from

Russia, Sweden, and Italy were in the room. Someone was screaming with joy. They all clapped until their hands were red and stinging.

In the new DOS headquarters at Belgrade City Assembly, Bojan Bosiljcic appeared on the television screen saying "New Radio Television Serbia." He and Miodrag Zupanc had just come up with the name in Kosutnjak.

A few moments earlier, in the restaurant of the RTS building at Kosutnjak, eight people had put their signature to a sheet of lined paper. It was headed "Editorial staff of RTS, October 5, 2000." At the bottom: "Belgrade, October 5, 2000, 11:40 P.M."

Covic, sitting at the same table, was writing the speech he planned to read to the audience as the first guest of the New RTS. Djindjic was later to describe this address to the nation as "a piece of pure statesmanship."

Shortly afterward, Buha's men arrived at the building. Petar Lazovic, unprepared, nearly died of fright.

That same night, Vojislav Kostunica was a guest on the first program presented by New RTS. Nenad Ristic was finally satisfied. "If Kostunica had gone to any other television station I don't know what would have happened to us," said the new RTS director, giving his account for this book.

At three in the morning the first new television news was broadcast. Petar Lazovic was back in the studio again after almost ten years. No one else would have done. Lazovic had been in the studio in 1966 when Josip Broz, "Tito," sacked the top policeman of Yugoslavia, Aleksandar Rankovic. He was there again when Soviet troops invaded Czechoslovakia in August 1968. And when the Israeli-Egyptian war broke out in 1973. He was also one of the first to break the news when Tito died. When the revolution happened in Romania in 1989, Lazovic was again on duty. "I just seem to catch this kind of stuff," he said.

Ivica Stojkovic told his wife later: "You can't imagine how happy I was to be in the program control room! After so many years!"

TWENTY-FIVE

HÔTEL DE VILLE

"We've crossed the bridge and there's no way back," Co-President of New Serbia Milan St. Protic thought to himself hours earlier when he was the first of the Democratic Opposition of Serbia (DOS) leaders to enter the Belgrade City Assembly. The creation of a new state had begun in Belgrade at that moment. For St. Protic, the symbolism was more than significant: Revolution—Bastille—City Assembly. "Hôtel de Ville!" he thought, and walked into the Belgrade City Assembly.

The Hôtel de Ville, the Assembly of the City of Paris, was the epicenter of the French Revolution. It was there that the citizens of Paris armed themselves on July 14, 1789, before setting out for the Bastille. The Marquis de Launay, the governor of the Bastille was killed. "That's insurrection," said the king. "No, Sire," one of his courtiers replied. "That's revolution!"

Three months later, on October 5, 1789, the women of Paris, followed by twenty thousand members of Lafayette's National Guard, set out from the Hôtel de Ville on the 12-mile road to Versailles and the king. Drunk and out of control, they attempted to kill the queen. On the morning of October 6, the king was brought to Paris. "It's over!" wrote De Moulin.

Three years later, on August 9, 1792, the first seeds of what would become the Reign of Terror under the Jacobins were planted in the Hôtel de Ville. The City Administration of Paris, representing 30 of the 48 Paris districts, proclaimed the revolutionary Commune. The following day they marched on the Tuileries. Louis was deposed and later executed and the monarchy abolished.

"Mother of God!" thought St. Protic. "What have I got myself mixed up in?" Other representatives of the revolution soon arrived at the City Assembly. In front of the building the mob pushed in.

Democratic Opposition of Serbia had seized power in the streets. This kind of poetic justice has happened all through history. Those who win power in the streets lose it in the streets. Milosevic had based his power on the enormous rallies that propelled him to the leadership of Serbia in the late 1980s. It was only three years from the time the mob carried Andronicus I into the palace until the same rabble carried him out again and crucified him in the Constantinople hippodrome. As he died he muttered, "God have mercy! Why are you doing this to a broken reed?"

Milosevic didn't fare quite as badly. But in Belgrade that night they all wanted to tear him to pieces: the people in the squares, sections of the defecting establishment, police who feared reprisals for what he would see as treason, DOS leaders who wanted to "cut off the snake's head." None of them would have cared if Milosevic had ended up in the hippodrome. Months earlier, Nenad Canak, the leader of the League of Social Democrats, had promised Milosevic that he would end on the gallows if he tampered with the will of the people. "Kill yourself and save Serbia, Slobodan," they'd been singing for nearly a year at every big event in Serbia. Now the mob below the balcony of the Belgrade City Assembly was demanding that the dictator be arrested.

The former president could thank his lucky stars on October 5. Three things saved him: confusion in the ranks of DOS, the lack of any contingency plan for his arrest, and the fact that the new president, Kostunica, was a stickler for legality. He wanted an orderly state, continuity of government, and democratic procedures. On October 5 he wasn't interested in arresting the dictator.

Canak, who had been the most threatening of all of them, wasn't in Belgrade.

Kostunica arrived with Goran Svilanovic and Bishop Atanasije Rakita. They drove from the Patriarchate to the Nikola Tesla Secondary School on Narodnog Fronta Street. From there they walked to the Parliament. Kostunica addressed the people from the balcony of the City Assembly.

"Dear Serbia," said Kostunica at the end of his speech that evening, while the mob in the square called for a march on the suburb of Dedinje and Milosevic's head on a platter, "we're not going to march on Dedinje. We're going to stay here. We're going to stay here because these are the people's institutions, the assemblies, one, two, three of them. This is where we're staying because these are ours. And tonight, we're going to stay together to the end. You're going to stay with me, and I'm going to stay with you!"

"I thought it very important to begin establishing a new government with the least possible delay," Kostunica said for this book. "We had to demonstrate that we could exercise power, while the others couldn't. I was thinking of convening the Federal Parliament and the City Assembly and I mentioned this in my address from the balcony. I called on the representatives who had been elected to the Chamber of the Citizens and the Chamber of the Republics to come to the City Assembly, because we couldn't use the Federal Parliament building."

It wasn't practical. The representatives from Montenegro, still unsure of what had happened, neither could nor would come to Belgrade. The City Assembly was much easier. The councillors simply walked up from the square in front of the building. Sixty-five of them gathered on the first floor. Branko Belic, a Democratic Party representative and the eldest of those present, chaired the meeting. The first decision was that the ballot would not be secret.

To St. Protic it still seemed "totally revolutionary." He was elected mayor by acclamation, with none of the minutes or other customary documents. "There was an idea later on," said St. Protic, "to do all that retroactively, but I refused. I was elected in a revolutionary manner and that should neither be concealed nor falsified."

Kostunica was satisfied. The continuity of government had been established. Shortly afterward, the Crisis Center was set up in the mayor's office.

At about 5 P.M., the telephone rang in the G17 Plus office. Predrag Markovic picked it up. "This is the office of President Milutinovic," someone said, from the office of Serbia's President. "You wanted to talk to the president. He's ready."

"We wanted no such thing," Markovic answered curtly and hung up. Some things just didn't seem possible, even on October 5.

Only then did he begin to wonder. "I don't suppose, by any chance, that anyone asked to talk to Milutinovic?" he asked.

"I did," said Mladjan Dinkic. "It was just a joke, really, as we passed the Presidency."

The telephone rang again. "Thank God," thought Markovic.

Milan Milutinovic was indeed ready to talk. He set one condition, that the delegation coming to meet him should include Mijat Damjanovic, the director of the Center for Public and Local Administration, a member of the G17 Council and a former associate. They had trained together in the same swimming club 40 years earlier. He also asked for Slobodan Vucetic, a former judge of the Constitutional Court of Serbia.

Unfortunately neither of them was there. Nor did anybody know where they were. They had been with Dinkic in front of the Federal Parliament, and no one had seen them since the assault on the Parliament began. Their cell phones were switched off. G17 Plus sent out a search party.

Damjanovic and Vucetic were located while Markovic was at the Tanjug news agency. Milutinovic wasn't fully aware of how things stood. He suggested meeting either at his home in Dedinje or at the presidency in Pioneer Park. They explained that coming to the presidency probably wasn't a good idea. "All right," said Milutinovic, "then you can come to me. I'll send a car for you."

The G17 Plus people politely refused. Driving through Belgrade in a black government car that day would have been like playing Russian roulette. It was in any case highly unlikely that the vehicle would be able to cross downtown to the G17 Plus office. Predrag Markovic was shouting "Let him send a car, but make it an old Yugo!"

So Mijat Damjanovic and Slobodan Vucetic set off in their own car to see Milutinovic. Bozo Prelevic, a former judge who would soon be co-minister for police in the Serbian government, followed. He stayed outside while the others entered Milutinovic's house. Kostunica thought that contact should be established with the former authorities in order to avoid violent conflict. Djindjic feared a counterattack by the army, paramilitary groups, and parts of the police. This was the reason for setting up the Crisis Center in the Belgrade City Assembly, the first body established by the new government in Serbia.

Damjanovic and Vucetic didn't have much success. At 11 P.M. Milutinovic left them in his house and went "to talk to The Man." At 11:55 he sent word that he still hadn't managed to see him. At midnight they left his house and returned downtown.

Djindjic was convinced that a counterattack was imminent. Kostunica thought that even if Milosevic managed to stay in power as an illegal president he wouldn't last long. "He can't stay as an illegal president," Djindjic said to him, "he'd have us all killed."

Kostunica left the Crisis Center.

The rest of them decided to organize the defense. There were more than 300 people in and around the City Assembly with rifles.

Captain Dragan deployed his men with Wasps on Kneza Milosa Street.

All access routes to the city that could be used by troops were guarded by men with heavy weapons.

The new government's longest night had begun. Most of the new leaders expected the strike to occur between three and four in the morning. Kostunica didn't believe there would be one.

Svilanovic was assigned to the media in the Crisis Center, Vuk Obradovic to the police, and Momcilo Perisic to the army. The Belgrade police asked for negotiations. The people were seizing weapons from the police station on Majke Jevrosime Street.

Kostunica went to RTS. A state based on the idea of a constitution needed a state television network.

"Once the media were in our hands a dispute began over who should go where," said Kostunica. "Some of them suggested I go to TV Politika, some to Studio B because they had been the first to defect to the people. But as soon as I saw that New RTS had begun broadcasting I decided to go to them. This was a symbolic act for me: The new president of the Federal Republic of Yugoslavia, the new head of state addressing the nation on the state television network. Then it really became the state television: until then it had only been Party television."

The president of Yugoslavia drove to New RTS in Kosutnjak in the same car that supporters of Slobodan Milosevic had battered during the election campaign in Kosovska Mitrovica. The old RTS had presented this as proof that the people were against Kostunica. It broadcast footage of Kostunica being pelted with eggs and stones, accompanying it with a malicious commentary. Now, at New RTS, he was greeted with applause.

At the same time, Boris Tadic, who would soon become minister for communications, sent word that the first issue of the new *Politika* was ready. "It's over!" thought Djindjic. *Politika* was a symbol. Djindjic was confident that once the paper appeared in the morning, with the front page screaming "Revolution!" Milosevic would be unable to strike back.

The first issue of the new *Politika* didn't scream "Revolution!" from the headlines. It looked like any other edition of the paper, continuing the long-standing tradition of a front-page headline beginning "Yugoslav President . . ." But this time, the name of the president had changed. "Yugoslav President Vojislav Kostunica . . ." it read.

"That was the greatest shock for me," Kostunica said later. "I couldn't believe it." He spent half that night and the following day autographing copies of *Politika*.

TWENTY-SIX

TANKS!

The DOS sent Belgrade mayor Milan St. Protic to the police station on Majke Jevrosime Street. It had been ruined by the time he got there. "It was full of people," he said later, "and no police anywhere to be seen. They were picking it clean, taking anything they could get hold of."

On one of the upper floors of the building St. Protic found a policeman in civilian clothes shaking like a leaf. "He couldn't even explain to me where the weapons were."

St. Protic and his men calmed him down. Then the policeman led them to the armory at the very top of the building. St. Protic was horrified by what he found there. "Automatic rifles, machine guns, Wasps. It was terrible!"

According to police records, the weapons on issue to the station included 300 automatic rifles, 16 machine guns, 19 Scorpions, and 260 pistols. There was a total of more than 700 firearms.

There was only one thing St. Protic could do. "Out! Out!" he shouted at the top of his lungs. His security guards managed to drive the mob out. In front of the station St. Protic made a speech: "You're not fighting Milosevic here. You're fighting him up there, in the square!" he told them. "Come on, let's all go there!" He left his security guards in front of the station. The weapons were later moved to the City Assembly. Democratic Opposition of Serbia was building its own arsenal.

Goran Svilanovic went completely unarmed to negotiate. He set off with Momcilo Perisic and Sveta Djurdjevic for the city police headquarters on 29th November Street. They crossed the city on foot. At the corner of Cetinjska and 29th November Streets they met Maki. He was leading a cheerful crowd through the streets. "I've conquered the police!" he told them. The girl beside him was wearing a police general's cap.

The revolutionary from Valjevo seemed out of control. After RTS was conquered, his first thought had been to head for Dedinje. Then he realized there was an even better target which should have fallen earlier according to his personal schedule for the day: the huge city police headquarters. He managed to assemble 500 people at the square in front of the Parliament.

They were marching through the city waving their clubs and shouting victory. Maki was in front, a pistol tucked into his belt. The guys with the backpacks were making Molotov cocktails. Only the asphalt and the electric street lights distinguished them from pictures of the Revolution in Paris. The police officers couldn't believe their eyes when they arrived.

There were no more than 300 people inside the police building. A number of these were deployed in an internal courtyard. The rest were watching from behind the curtains as Maki's troops arrived. He called for negotiations. He sent men to all sides of the building with the same orders: "When I start, set fire to it!"

A police general came out of the building. "Give yourself up," Maki told him calmly.

"In what way?" asked the general.

The revolutionary thought about it.

"Give me something as proof of your surrender," he said.

The general handed over his cap.

"And that was all?" Svilanovic asked.

"That was all," said Maki.

The DOS negotiators continued on to the city police. Maki continued to celebrate. He'd conquered the police, he didn't need to conquer anything else.

The police took the DOS people more seriously. The truth was they recognized Sveta Djurdjevic and wanted to meet him. After he, Svilanovic, and Perisic waited in a reception area for some time, they were ushered in to see Branko Djuric. "The meeting didn't take long," Svilanovic said later. "We told him we'd do our best to restrain the mob from looting and crime and asked them to pledge that they wouldn't attack the people. That was all."

The DOS delegation also asked to be put in direct contact with Vlajko Stojiljkovic. Momcilo Perisic spoke by telephone to the police minister, who recited a litany of the criminal acts committed by the revolutionaries. "He still hadn't grasped the situation," said Svilanovic.

"Tanks!" The story spread like wildfire through Belgrade. "Tanks!" DOS headquarters in the City Assembly was told about them. "Tanks!" the people of the Jajinci neighborhood were alarmed. They pushed a couple of Yugo cars and some garbage containers onto the Avala road.

"The tanks did leave the barracks at Bubanj Potok on Thursday, October 5, at 10 P.M.," said General Pavkovic, "but only to go to their base in Vozdovac. They were ordered to take back roads, through Jajinci. Nobody in the army is insane enough to send tanks out against the people. That's not what they're for. We wouldn't even think about anything like Tiananmen Square in Belgrade."

The people in DOS weren't so sure. When it came to the army, they weren't sure about anything. "It was a black box to us," Djindjic said later. "No information at all."

Momcilo Perisic got on the phone, without much success. The only thing he learned was that there were cells in the military prison reserved for Kostunica and Svilanovic. The military prosecutor had actually filed criminal complaints against the two DOS leaders the day before for taking out newspaper advertisements. In one advertisement, Svilanovic appealed to his former wartime colleagues-in-arms, both officers and other ranks, not to fire at the people. The other, less significant, was over the signature "The Democratic Opposition of Serbia—Dr. Vojislav Kostunica," the formal title of the DOS election ticket. After October 5, nothing more was heard about these charges.

That evening at the City Assembly, the threat of a military prison didn't seem real to Svilanovic. He proposed taking a car and visiting a few barracks. During the wars he had been with the First Armored Brigade, stationed in Vozdovac.

"We got into a City Assembly jeep and went on tour," said Svilanovic later. "We went to the Military Medical Academy barracks in Banjica, to the July 4 barracks in Vozdovac, to Trosarina. There were Caterpillar tracks in front of the Vozdovac barracks, but we didn't see any tanks."

Perisic's phone calls had still yielded no results. The man sent to the registration room at the Vozdovac barracks came back without any new information. The man Perisic had sent him to see wasn't there.

Djindjic was still at the City Assembly, still apprehensive. Actors and politicians were making speeches from the balcony. The people had been asked to stay all night in front of the Assembly. This seemed to be the best defense.

Then the Russian ambassador announced that the Russian foreign minister, Igor Ivanov, wanted to come to Belgrade in the morning to meet Vojislav Kostunica.

"You mean Yugoslav President Vojislav Kostunica?" the DOS people asked the Kremlin on the phone, ten minutes later.

"Yes," came the reply.

Kostunica wanted to go to bed. At home, for the first time that day, he felt afraid. "I was away from the crowd for the first time that evening. While we were in the City Assembly it was still protecting us in some way. At home, I was alone. For the first time I was aware of the danger, that it might be better to stay awake." The fatigue was stronger than the fear. He forced himself to close his eyes.

TWENTY-SEVEN

BOSKO BUHA, OUTLAW

Bosko Buha had good reason to be satisfied. By the morning, his entire brigade, to the last man, was in the barracks—even the men on leave, on sick leave, and the ones seconded to the police station in Volgina Street. He had a total of 300 men on the morning of October 6. "I could march on Tirana, let alone No. 29," he thought happily.

Everything was still going his way. G17 Plus had called: "Anything you need, money, food, petrol, just let us know and we'll get it to you straightaway." The barracks stores were full. A cook from the Ministry of Internal Affairs had defected to Buha. "I'm with you," he'd said. On top of all that, he'd met Legija that morning.

The television had brought them together. The brigade had made an announcement on New RTS the night before to state "who we were and where we were," Buha said later, "just to let the people know, so they would be ready to help us if needed."

Obviously Milorad ("Legija") Ulemek had been watching New RTS. Buha was just what he needed. His brigade was one of the strongest police units, the kind you'd like beside you if there was any mess.

"Legija sent me," a mutual friend said to Buha. "Do you want to meet him?" Buha was delighted. The commander of the Special Operations Unit appeared at Trebevicka Street at 9 A.M.

"We threw our arms around each other," Buha said later, "and asked each other how things were. We'd known each other in Kosovo and we were in agreement immediately. If anybody attacked him, I'd be there, and if anybody attacked me, he'd be there. There'd be nothing any of the police could do to us. We were too strong a force."

Buha called his troops together. They fell in, wearing full gear and weapons, on the huge parade ground in front of the barracks, arrayed in a "U" shape. When the commander appeared they applauded him for two minutes. He knew what that meant. He stood them at ease and from the middle of the square told them what might happen. "We may have to fight, and we may get killed," he said. They liked the first part.

Later that day Vlajko Stojiljkovic proclaimed Bosko Buha a traitor and the Police Brigade a paramilitary group.

On Saturday morning, October 7, the central police headquarters on 29th November Street called the barracks. The head of the Police Directorate, Colonel Milos Vojinovic, wanted to know if he could come to see Buha. "Yes, he can," Buha's aide relayed the message, "at 11 o'clock." Vojinovic was Buha's superior.

"Nothing much happened," Buha said later. "He arrived, there was some small talk about politics. We're normal people, he knows me, he knows my deputy. Then Branko Djuric called. 'Let's meet for coffee,' he said. 'Okay,' I told him. There was no longer anything to be afraid of." But he left orders for his deputy, just in case: "If you don't hear from me by then, call out the men and go get them."

"Understood," replied Vladimir Ilic.

At the central police headquarters, they asked Buha politely over coffee to take charge of security for Kostunica's inauguration.

The next day, at the Ministry of Internal Affairs, he met with General Vlastimir Djordjevic, Legija, Colonel Nikola Curcic of the anti-terrorist unit, and the colonel from the green room. They proposed Djordjevic as liaison officer for the four units. Democratic Opposition of Serbia wanted it done legally. With Djordjevic consenting, it was. One of the key people in the Serbian Ministry of Internal Affairs, the chief of the Public Security Section, was now on their side.

Stojiljkovic proclaimed him a traitor too. The denunciation, which until a couple of days before had meant certain dismissal, and perhaps even death, was now meaningless. Djordjevic continued working.

"We weren't rebels or Indians trying to overthrow generals and governments," the colonel from the green room said later. "We just wanted to see that justice was done."

When it was over, Buha was content. His son was still a Red Star fan after all.

✴ ✴ ✴

It was important to get through the night. Milder stayed beside his bus the whole time. Gigo and Sekula hopped from square to square. Bubac met his best friend from Topola in Pioneer Park. "We stuck it to them!" they both shouted together. They hugged and clapped each other on the back, the Serbian greeting.

"Where did you attack from?" asked Bubac.

"Mount Kosmaj."

"I came from the Morava."

They spent the night in a café. Belgrade's cafés were open all night. It was a carnival, and no one was worried about anything but celebrating. For them, the job was finished. They began to disperse before dawn.

Igor, Velja Ilic's bodyguard, was furious. He got into the car and set off for Cacak. He was the odd man out. He'd wanted to storm the government of Serbia and the Presidency. He wanted to arrest Milosevic. When he left he didn't even report to Velja. "We had the opportunity to get rid of Milosevic and all those generals, and we blew it. I was terribly disappointed," he said later. "I just got into the Volkswagen Golf and drove away." Three more of Velja's men left with him.

The rest of the Cacak people left Belgrade a little later. They had one more thing to do before they left. At six in the morning, when Belgraders began driving to work, they blocked the intersection of Takovska Street and Kosovska Street with a truck. A few cars stopped. "Out!" they ordered. "Get out of the car and stay there!" The revolution still had to be defended. The people of Cacak, who hadn't taken their shoes off for three days, thought they were entitled to a replacement.

The buses from Kraljevo followed the ones from Cacak. The people of Novi Sad were already at home celebrating. The Lazendic brothers were drinking the vodka they'd "captured" from the Federal Parliament. "Well," said their uncle. "Wasn't that something!"

The exodus was a problem for the revolution. Ceda Jovanovic was shouting from the balcony of the City Assembly. "Don't leave! Do you really think Milosevic is asleep?" Radio Indeks reporter Jovan Palavestra left anyway, confident that the change had happened. In the early morning light, Belgrade looked to him like a battleground that hadn't been cleared. "From the Parliament to the Vuk Karadzic Monument I couldn't see a single garbage container standing upright. There was rubbish everywhere." It was a warm, sunny morning. This journalist, accustomed to reporting from the sultry streets of Belgrade, felt strange on his way home. It was the first time he'd reported a victory.

Milan St. Protic was sitting in the mayor's office at the City Assembly with Ruzica Djindjic and Ljiljana Lucic, Democratic Party official, complaining about the diminishing crowd under the balcony. By seven in the morning there were only a few hundred people left. Belgrade was quiet again. Then there was a roar: "Tanks!" St. Protic thought, suddenly frightened. The two women turned pale. The mayor's office was suddenly full of people running toward the windows. The sound was coming from Terazije Square.

Milan St. Protic has forgotten how long they stood there, lined up at the windows like sparrows. He only remembers the moment when a vast mass of marchers with drums and trumpets appeared from Terazije, where they'd been hidden by the buildings. They turned toward the City Assembly. The replacements had arrived for the small, tired crowd under the balcony. "They took an hour to pass," said St. Protic later. "It was over!"

Vojislav Kostunica woke up exactly an hour later. When he got out of bed he wasn't just the president of Yugoslavia. "I was a president of Yugoslavia who had to meet the Russian foreign affairs minister," he said later. He set off on foot to his party headquarters.

The doors to the massive Federal Government building in New Belgrade had yet to be opened. The Russian Foreign Ministry was advised that the venue for the meeting between the two statesmen had still not been set. Zvonimir Trajkovic, who had been an adviser to Milosevic in the early 1990s and was now working for Kostunica, was on the phone. At 11 A.M., Kostunica entered the Federal Government building. At 11:45 A.M. the Russian delegation was told that the meeting would take place there. A short time later the new president and the Russian foreign minister held a joint press conference.

"Getting into that building was very important," said the Yugoslav president. "It signified the takeover of power."

Kostunica set up his office in a large, cold suite of rooms that he would move out of a few days later. Electric heaters kept him and his advisers warm. A few hours later he was told that the Constitutional Court of Yugoslavia had ruled that he was officially the president of Yugoslavia. The decision had already been published in the *Government Gazette*. The first copies of the

Gazette had been distributed at 1 A.M. on October 6. The Constitutional Court, apparently without Milosevic's knowledge, had decided to desert the man who had given them their orders up until then. Fear of the dictator had gone up in flames with the Parliament, and now he was alone. The people who had condescended to keep him company had floated off on the waves of the revolution. The judges of the Constitutional Court had boarded a lifeboat. There was no further fear of retaliation from Milosevic.

There were only two more dramas to be played out before the end.

TWENTY-EIGHT

THE ARMY VERSUS STATE SECURITY

Some of the men of the Sixty-Third Paratroop Brigade and a group of officers from the special police forces, their commander included, ran into each other in a Belgrade café early on the evening on October 6. Both groups had simply gone there for a drink.

"Well," said the colonel, looking up from the table, "are you going to attack us?"

The paratroopers laughed.

The colonel ordered a round of drinks.

He raised his glass to them. "Let us know if you are, and we'll go somewhere else."

"Okay," said the paratroopers, "but you tell us when you want to attack, so that we can go somewhere else, too."

It all sounded friendly. But it wasn't. The elite military troops and the police who had gone over to DOS were both looking down the barrel of a gun. Army chief of staff Pavkovic had ordered the Seventy-Second Brigade to surround the Institute for Security in Banjica, which housed the State Security Special Operations Units under their commander, Legija. Buha put his men on full alert and set out to help Legija. The colonel rang General Staff and left a message for Pavkovic: "Don't do anything foolish!" Pavkovic sent armored vehicles with twin 30 mm cannons to the Institute.

It was easy for such a situation to develop in the interregnum which ensued in the first days after October 5. Only two institutions of the new system were functioning: Kostunica and the City Assembly. All the institutions of the old regime were falling apart.

The two armed forces had both lost their chain of command. They were wary of each other and nervous about what the final outcome of these events would be. So they engaged in saber rattling. Rade Markovic, then head of Serbia's State Security Service, puts it all down to a logical error. "After the events at the Parliament and RTS, we began to establish contact with DOS," said Markovic. "It was as simple as that. The unrest, the break-ins at police stations, and the fires had to be stopped. It didn't do anybody any good. So the Service sent messages and people to the DOS leaders to put an end to it. And that's where the problem arose."

Before, during, and after October 5, the security services were keeping a check on each other. Military intelligence sources kept Pavkovic informed about their contacts, and quite possibly about Legija's meetings with Zoran Djindjic on October 4 and 5. Military intelligence came to the conclusion that Legija was no longer taking orders from Rade Markovic and might attack the General Staff. Their reasons for thinking that remain unknown. General Pavkovic called Markovic, the chief of the Serbian State Security Service. They agreed to meet in the General Staff headquarters, the entrance to which is little more than a hundred yards away from State Security head-quarters. Their two huge compounds even share a common boundary. It was after midnight when Markovic set out from the Institute for Security. There were still no guns to be seen across the fence.

"What's going on at State Security?" asked Pavkovic.

"Nothing," replied Markovic, "we're trying to calm things down."

"You no longer have command of the Special Operations Units," said the army chief.

"That's not true," replied the head of State Security. "The units have not been given any illegal or unreasonable orders, and they haven't disobeyed any orders. Whatever orders I have given them have been carried out."

"That's not true," retorted Pavkovic. "They want to attack the General Staff!"

Giving his account for this book when everything was over, Markovic described Pavkovic's belief as an understandable mistake. "It wasn't realistic to expect that the Special Operations Units, which are basically a small force, would attack the army which is so much more powerful. Also the General Staff was very well guarded and there was additional security brought in during the evening. The army spent the whole night moving its units to protect its buildings and other facilities."

Pavkovic didn't believe him. He asked for Legija to come in to the General Staff. Markovic made the phone call. The commander appeared ten minutes later, with an escort. The three of them had known one another for a long time, and well enough. They didn't want to quarrel. Pavkovic ordered a table to be set for dinner. The small room in the General Staff Headquarters was freshly painted in white. It was neat, military, with new period-style cabinets and a matching table. The three officers ate and exchanged promises—but not until the chief of the General Staff had made a few threats between mouthfuls. "It's your choice," Pavkovic said. "If you advance against the army we'll defend ourselves with all our resources." He added, "And your two combat helicopters can't take off from your base without our clearance." Then they pledged there would be no conflict.

Markovic and Legija left the General Staff confident that all their problems were solved. "I thought that they understood that it was all because of poor communication."

But Pavkovic saw it differently. "When they left," he said, speaking for this book, "I ordered certain measures to be taken. I also had some units brought to Belgrade, part of the Sixty-Third and a section of the Seventy-Second." Two huge Andonovs landed at Batajnica airport, giving rise to a rumor, which spread like wildfire through a Belgrade eager to hear good news, that Milosevic was fleeing. Heavily armed paratroopers ran from the freight planes and leapt into trucks. At 3 A.M., Markovic was informed that the Security Institute was partly surrounded. Gun barrels could be seen over the neighboring gate. "We were partly surrounded by armored vehicles, and their guns were aimed at us," Markovic said later.

One of the Red Berets, laughing, told a friend on the phone, "Come over here and see what these Partizans are doing!"

Inside the Security Institute, Markovic told Legija, the commander of the Special Operations Units, that he would take care of the problem himself. The colonel from the green room rang the General Staff. Buha was prepared to help.

"We came to an exceptionally good understanding with Pavkovic," Markovic testified for this book. "When the matter was raised at a meeting with the president of the state, he admitted that there was probably no truth in their information."

This was very likely the key. In the days following October 5, all the actors in the drama placed themselves under the direction of the new head of state. Milorad "Legija" Ulemek went to the federal government building and took an oath before Kostunica. Rade Markovic went there and addressed Kostunica as "Mr. President." Pavkovic telephoned from the General Staff:

"Congratulations on your victory, Mr. President," he said. "Under the Constitution you command the army in both war and peace. I am placing myself and the entire army at your disposal."

The paratroopers withdrew from their position.

TWENTY-NINE

MILOSEVIC RECEIVES KOSTUNICA

One more thing still needed to happen. Before the conflict among the military elite, before the siege, before Kostunica's victory was recognized, before all of that, someone else had something to do.

Slobodan Milosevic had to concede defeat.

General Nebojsa Pavkovic was the mediator in this. At about 6 P.M. on October 6, President Kostunica's new office called the General Staff. "Can you organize a meeting with Milosevic?" they asked the general.

"I'll try," replied Pavkovic. He rang the former president.

"Out of the question," said Milosevic.

Fifteen minutes later he rang Pavkovic back.

"All right," he said, "but here at my house, no witnesses, no waiters. Only him and me."

Pavkovic called the federal government building.

"No," they said at President Kostunica's office. "It should be here."

"Out of the question," Milosevic said again when he got the message.

Half an hour later, Pavkovic was told that Kostunica insisted on the meeting.

"Out of the question." Milosevic, at the end of his tether, deserted and impotent, still wouldn't give in.

They tried once more from the president's office. Pavkovic, still mediating, gave him the message.

"Kostunica proposes that I attend the meeting."

And the same curt reply from Milosevic: "Out of the question."

It seemed the idea wasn't going to work. Then Pavkovic tried something else.

"Would you like me to go to Kostunica and invite him to come to you?"

"All right," replied the lonely dictator.

At about 8 P.M., a handful of military vehicles pulled up in front of the federal government building. "It was very strange," said President Kostunica later. He got into the vehicle almost alone. Journalist Milos Jevtovic, a go-between in negotiations between Kostunica and the army, was his only escort. When they found out about it the DOS people were rigid with fear. For Kostunica, on October 6, to be at the mercy of the army in one of their vehicles didn't seem like a good idea. If anything happened to the new president, the revolution would not only have lost its mascot, but would also be left without the only institution it had managed to conquer. "I was confident," Kostunica said later. "I have always had confidence in the army. Also I trusted Jevtovic's judgment. He thought we should go."

Milosevic met them on Uzicka Street. He welcomed them, "as a good host would," said Pavkovic. Kostunica gave his impression: "I was going to him for the first time. I was thinking about it as we entered the house. I was thinking that opposition people had been to see him before, but always as opposition. I was coming as the man in power."

Two presidents and a general entered a sitting room. Milosevic was waiting for Kostunica to begin the conversation. Kostunica was looking at General Pavkovic. "Well, here we are," said the general. A minute or two later he left the room.

The conversation lasted for an hour. No record, no witnesses. Later, giving his account for this book, Kostunica said that they disagreed only on two points. Milosevic claimed at first that his term of office, regardless of the election results, would not finish until July 2001. He also complained about the violence in the streets, citing the burning of a district chief's house in Leskovac and of his son's perfume shop in Belgrade's Terazije Square.

Much later, in Skopje, the new president spoke to Richard Holbrooke, the U.S. ambassador to the United Nations, about Milosevic, saying that he had accused him of only one thing that evening. "I told him that he had spent hours and days talking to you but he had never spoken to the opposition in his own country at all."

Holbrooke grinned. "Well, that's right," he said.

As soon as Kostunica mentioned the ruling of the Constitutional Court, the discussion was over. "If that's the case, then it's another matter," said Milosevic. "I haven't seen it, but if that's the case, then I concede."

"I was surprised," said the new president. "I don't know whether he really hadn't heard about the Constitutional Court's ruling, but the gesture itself surprised me."

They bade farewell to each other cordially. "If you'd done that a day earlier," thought Pavkovic, "none of this would have happened."

The former president insisted that Pavkovic stay at Uzicka Street. Milos Jevtovic insisted that the general should escort the new president back to the federal government building. "I brought them here, it's only decent that I take them back," said Pavkovic.

The general and the president had coffee together in the Federal Government building, then Pavkovic returned to Uzicka Street.

"There's nothing further for me here, General," said Milosevic. "The election results have been published in the *Government Gazette*. All I can do is congratulate Kostunica and sign the documents. Do you have the telephone number?"

Vojislav Kostunica was on Pozeska Street, hurrying to his second interview ever with RTS. His cell phone rang.

"I shall appear on television," said Milosevic, "if you agree. I shall mention the election results and congratulate you publicly."

"I agree," said the president of Yugoslavia. He put the cell phone back in his pocket.

EPILOGUE

This time, Milosevic kept his word. At 10:39 P.M. on October 6, he appeared on the YU Info Channel and announced that he had just received the ruling of the Constitutional Court that Vojislav Kostunica was the new president of Yugoslavia.

The people who had voted for Kostunica had done him a favor, he said: he would now have plenty of time to play with his grandson Marko. "Well, he's giving us a laugh," said a fourteen-year-old named Jovana as she watched. The furious dictator looked terrible. His underlying desire for revenge made his recitation look like pure malice. For the first time in 13 years, Milosevic was helpless.

That Friday night, in the street, President Kostunica was puzzled. "What's going on?" he asked himself, then thought, "There must have been a football match." Only later did he realize that the people in the streets were celebrating Milosevic's acknowledgment of his defeat, the miracle that many believed wouldn't happen during their lifetime.

Democratic Party President Djindjic was still busy with the revolution. As yet they had only the president of Yugoslavia and the media. The police were still wavering. And what about the secret police, the army, the Serbian government, the National Bank, the customs service, the post office, and all the large public companies? They were all still intact. He went to Kostunica with his suggestions for the next move. He had in mind the way Trotsky had taken over the lifeblood of the state on October 24, 1917, while Lenin was in hiding and Stalin was still wondering when the right time would be to start the revolution. With Djindjic's blessing, DOS took over the National Bank of Yugoslavia and the Federal Customs Administration. On Saturday, October 7, President Kostunica went to the Serbian Ministry of Internal Affairs and spoke to the defeated "military leader" Vlajko Stojiljkovic. That evening he called on Nebojsa Pavkovic, the chief of the General Staff. He'd learned another lesson from the Red October of 1917: Don't attack the government until you're sure the army won't defend it.

Kostunica wanted legality. His model was Louis Bonaparte's Eighteenth Brumaire. "Bonaparte's logic ruled out violence. But the situation had to be brought to an end. Thus it was necessary to resort to persuasion, to go to Council rooms and talk to deputies, to try politely to enforce parliamentary procedure," wrote Curzio Malaparte in his *Technique du coup d'état.*

It was Milan Milutinovic, the president of Serbia, who decided the course of the revolution. He again called G17 Plus on October 6. Kostunica could now put an end to the debate about the road the revolution should take. "I'm going to see Milutinovic," he told Djindjic. "My satisfaction that everything would proceed on a legal course outweighed my regret about having to stop halfway through," said the Democratic Party president.

On Saturday evening, Vojislav Kostunica was sworn in as president of Yugoslavia in front of the Yugoslav Parliament, meeting in the Sava Center. Among the people at the swearing-in were the Greek foreign minister, George Papandreou, and the Norwegian foreign minister, Thorbjørn Jagland. The whole world was crazy about Kostunica: The lifting of the international sanctions against Yugoslavia began and relations were reestablished with the European Union, the United Nations, France, Germany, Britain, and the United States. On December 1, on *Time*'s website, the president of Yugoslavia was the front-runner in the Person of the Year polls.

Milosevic's son, Marko, flew to Moscow on a false passport, his wife and child in tow.

On Monday, October 11, Slobodan Milosevic's Socialists, conscious of their own impotence, tried to salvage what they could: They agreed to cooperate with DOS in a caretaker Serbian government and to call early elections for the Serbian Parliament on December 23.

The defeated military leader, former Police Minister Vlajko Stojiljkovic, resigned as minister for internal affairs, unconvincingly invoking the incompatibility of his new role as a federal minister of Parliament with that of a minister in the Serbian government.

Zoran Djindjic was nominated by DOS as candidate for Serbian prime minister.

Sekula, the colonel from the green room, Igor, Bubac, Ivan, Gigo, and Milder got on with their lives. But now they felt better. They'd succeeded in doing the impossible.

Every book needs an ending. A four-year-old named Sophie, in her own way a co-author, knows how things turned out. "Sloba was smashed to bits," she said. "Barbie and the Power Rangers beat him." She had no further interest in the matter. "Here's your boring news," she said, leaving the room as the evening news appeared on the screen.

CHRONOLOGY

Sunday-Monday, September 24–25

Abortive attempt at an election night meeting between Vojislav Kostunica and Colonel Zivko Trajkovic, commander of the special anti-terrorist units of the Serbian Ministry of Internal Affairs.

Tuesday, September 26

Democratic Opposition of Serbia (DOS) decides to defend its election victory at any price if Slobodan Milosevic decides to tamper with the votes. "If he fires, we will fire" is the official DOS position. Kostunica is absent from the meeting when the vote takes place.

Tuesday, October 3

Agreement is reached on organizing the arrival of demonstrators in Belgrade in five convoys from five directions.

Wednesday, October 4

10 A.M. Vladimir Ilic, deputy commander of the Police Brigade from Belgrade, refuses to fire on striking miners at Kolubara.

NOON Colonel Bosko Buha, the commander of the Police Brigade, talks to the miners.

4 P.M. Protesters break through a police cordon on the bridge across the Kolubara River, on the road connecting the Kolubara mine to the Ibar Highway.

4:45 P.M. A senior Belgrade police officer is instructed to draw up a plan of defense for the Yugoslav and Serbian Parliaments, the Serbian Presidency, and Radio Television Serbia (RTS). The plan is completed at 11 P.M.

5 P.M. Vojislav Kostunica arrives at the Kolubara mine.

6 P.M. Zoran Djindjic, the president of the Democratic Party, meets Milorad "Legija" Ulemek, the commander of the Serbian State Security Service's Special Operations Unit, on Admirala Geprata Street.

Thursday, October 5

MIDNIGHT "Plan Three" is the order to use all available weapons to stop the convoys intending to converge on Belgrade. The colonel in the green room of the Serbian police, at 101 Kneza Milosa Street, is given the order. Cedomir Jovanovic, senior officer of the Democratic Party, calls the convoy leaders from the party headquarters on Proleterskih Brigada Street.

Bogoljub "Maki" Arsenijevic practices for revolution with Molotov cocktails at the Jojkic Canal.

Captain Dragan begins surreptitiously taking his men into the Beogradjanka building, planning to use them in a takeover of the radio and television station Studio B that afternoon.

12:30 A.M. Nebojsa Pavkovic, the chief of staff of the Yugoslav Army, goes to bed.

1 A.M. Zoran Djindjic meets a senior Serbian police officer.

6 A.M. Co-President of New Serbia Velimir ("Velja") Ilic addresses a rally in Cacak. His message is "Victory or death."

7 A.M. More than one thousand people—inclduing mates Bubac, Gigo, and Sekula—set out from Kraljevo for Belgrade in about ten buses and a hundred cars.

About two thousand people from Uzice set off in 24 buses and 135 cars.

7:15 A.M. From Cacak, 230 trucks and 52 buses leave for Belgrade with hundreds of cars. There are more than ten thousand people in the 14-mile convoy.

General Nebojsa Pavkovic enters the General Staff building.

7:45 A.M. Protesters from Kraljevo break through a police roadblock in the village of Milocaj.

8 A.M. Protesters from Cacak break through a roadblock near the village of Majdan.

8:45 A.M. Protesters from Cacak break through another roadblock, near the village of Celije.

9 A.M. About 1,300 people from Novi Sad—including Otpor (Resistance) activist and "domestic traitor" Stanko Lazendic, his brother, Milan, and his uncle— leave for Belgrade in 25 buses. A thousand more people are in about 250 cars.

9:15 A.M. The Novi Sad protesters rush through a police barricade at the motorway entrance outside the city.

10 A.M. Representatives of non-government organizations (NGOs) demand that lists be published of all people who have been arrested and that lawyers and families be immediately informed about arrests in the future. Dobrivoje Glavonjic, who heads the Belgrade Magistrates Court, agrees.

10:30 A.M. The head of the Serbian Orthodox Church, Patriarch Pavle, receives Milan St. Protic, who will become the mayor of Belgrade that night.

11:20 A.M. The Cacak protesters reach Nikola Pasic Square in front of the Yugoslav Parliament.

11:30 A.M. RTS Strike Committee decides to black out the state television network.

NOON Members of Otpor gather in the square in front of Belgrade University's philosophy department.

The DOS leaders meet.

12:10 P.M. Police use tear gas to repel the first assault on the Yugoslav Parliament by the Cacak protesters.

12:22 P.M. Protestors led by G17 Plus with a mobile stage leave Republic Square for the Parliament.

12:25 P.M. Ljubisav ("Joe") Djokic, in a bulldozer, with Milan the 71-year-old baker in tow, leads protesters from Belgrade's Pozeska Street toward the Yugoslav Parliament.

1:00 P.M. G17 Plus files criminal charges against the Federal Election Commission in the Belgrade Palace of Justice.

2:00 P.M. Police headquarters order Colonel Buha of the Belgrade Police Brigade to rush to Belgrade, leaving only one company of police at Kolubara.

2:10 P.M. Strikers disrupt the RTS program. Television screens are dark for a few minutes.

2:40 P.M. Police headquarters reports fifteen thousand people in front of the Yugoslav Parliament.

3:01 P.M. Police headquarters reports that there are now seventy thousand demonstrators. Journalists put the number at between five hundred thousand and seven hundred thousand.

3:15 P.M. Mladjan Dinkic leaves his business card at the Serbian Presidency with a message for the president, Milan Milutinovic, to call him.

3:32 P.M. The assault on the Yugoslav Parliament begins.

4:09 P.M. A police officer reports to headquarters that the Parliament has been taken.

4:17 P.M. Police headquarters calls for redeployment of forces in the Parliament. There is no reply from the field units.

4:23 P.M. The first assault on the RTS building on Takovska Street is repelled.

4:30 P.M. A police helicopter flies over the center of Belgrade in the area between the Parliament and RTS. An order to drop tear-gas canisters on the crowd is not carried out.

4:33 P.M. Police headquarters orders units in RTS to take "further action." Some police believe this was an order to fire at the demonstrators.

5:05 P.M. Milan Milutinovic's office calls G17 Plus to say that President Milutinovic of Serbia is ready to talk.

5.10 P.M. Demonstrators gather in front of the police station on Majke Jevrosime Street.

5:35 P.M. The Special Operations Unit of the State Security Service arrives in front of RTS. The troops salute the demonstrators and leave.

5:45 P.M. Police headquarters tell units in RTS to withdraw to base.

5:50 P.M. Probable time of the fall of the police station on Majke Jevrosime Street. (Police reports put it at 7:45 P.M. but this is incorrect.)

6:00 P.M. Police radio communications collapse. Headquarters stops working. Free Studio B begins broadcasting.

Zoran Djindjic meets State Security Service Milorad "Legija" Ulemek for the second time.

7:30 P.M. The liberated TV Politika goes on the air with the statement "Politika is a liberated national media company."

8:00 P.M. An assault begins on the Belgrade offices of the Socialist Party in Student Square.

8:20 P.M. Predrag Markovic from G17 Plus takes over the state news agency, Tanjug.

8:30 P.M. Vojislav Kostunica addresses the demonstrators from a balcony of the Belgrade City Assembly.

Goran Svilanovic, Sveta Djurdjevic, and Momcilo Perisic negotiate with the Belgrade police chief, General Branko Djuric, at his headquarters on 29th November Street.

Radio Belgrade's first program begins broadcasting.

Nebojsa Covic talks to members of the crack Seventy-Second Brigade of the Yugoslav Army when he comes across them near the RTS transmission center in Kosutnjak.

9:05 P.M. RTS runs the text "New Radio Television Serbia" on its screens.

9:10 P.M. The New RTS program begins.

10:00 P.M. Tanks from Bubanj Potok pass through Jajinci on the way to barracks in Vozdovac.

10:20 P.M. Mijat Damjanovic and Slobodan Vucetic from G17 Plus leave to meet Serbian President Milutinovic at his house.

11 P.M. Milutinovic leaves to talk to "The Man."

Demonstrators break into the Socialist Party offices in Student Square.

11:15 P.M. Milan St. Protic is declared mayor of Belgrade.

Friday, October 6

2 A.M. The Russian ambassador to Belgrade informs Vojislav Kostunica that Igor Ivanov, Russia's foreign minister, wants to call on him the next day.

9 A.M. Milorad "Legija" Ulemek, Bosko Buha, and police special unit commanders meet in Trebevicka Street. Milosevic's "Praetorian Guard" decide to listen to the DOS.

NOON Vojislav Kostunica receives the Russian foreign minister, Igor Ivanov.

9:30 P.M Vojislav Kostunica meets Slobodan Milosevic at Uzicka Street in Belgrade.

10 P.M. General Nebojsa Pavkovic meets Rade Markovic, head of Serbia's secret police, and Milorad "Legija" Ulemek.

10:39 P.M. Slobodan Milosevic makes a special appearance on YU Info Channel to acknowledge Vojislav Kostunica's victory in the election.

Saturday, October 7

3 A.M. Elite units of the Yugoslav Army (sections of the Sixty-Third and Seventy-Second Brigades) surround the headquarters of the Serbian State Security Service. Rade Markovic again goes to meet General Pavkovic.

8 P.M. Vojislav Kostunica is sworn in as president of Yugoslavia before the Yugoslav Parliament.

LIST OF PARTICIPANTS

Batic, Vladan: President of the Christian Democratic Party

Buha, Colonel Bosko: Commander of the Police Brigade

Cerovic, Slobodan: Serbian tourism minister and president of the Belgrade Committee of the Yugoslav Left

Civil Alliance: Human rights and anti-war organization akin to a political party

Covic, Nebojsa: Leader of opposition Democratic Alternative Party

Democratic Opposition of Serbia (DOS): Loose organization opposed to Milosevic

Dinkic, Mladjan: Executive director of G17 Plus

Djindjic, Zoran: Democratic Party president

Djordjevic, General Vlastimir: Head of Yugoslav public security

Ilic, Velimir: A leader of New Serbia

Ilic, Vladimir: Deputy to Colonel Bosko Buha

Ivanovic, Slobodan: Director of the Anlave Medical Clinic

Jovanovic, Cedomir "Ceda": Senior officer of the Democratic Party

Jovanovic, Juliana: Assistant editor-in-chief of Radio Television Serbia current affairs programming

Kostunica, Vojislav: Leader of the Democratic Party of Serbia who ran against Slobodan Milosevic and won the elections

Markovic, Radomir: Serbian State Security chief

Mihajlovic, Dusan: President of New Democracy

Milutinovic, Milan: Serbian president

Pajic, Slobodan: Head of Security for Nebojsa Covic

Pavkovic, General Nebojsa: Chief of Staff of the Yugoslav Army

Perisic, General Momcilo: Former chief of staff of the Yugoslav Army and head of the Movement for a Democratic Serbia

Ristic, Nenad: Former director of Radio Television Serbia

St. Protic, Milan: A leader of New Serbia

Stojiljkovic, Vlajko: Police Minister

Svilanovic, Goran: Leader of Civil Alliance

Ulemek, Milorad "Legija": Special Operations Commander, Chief of the "Red Berets"

Yugoslav Left: Communist party with staunchly anti-Western position

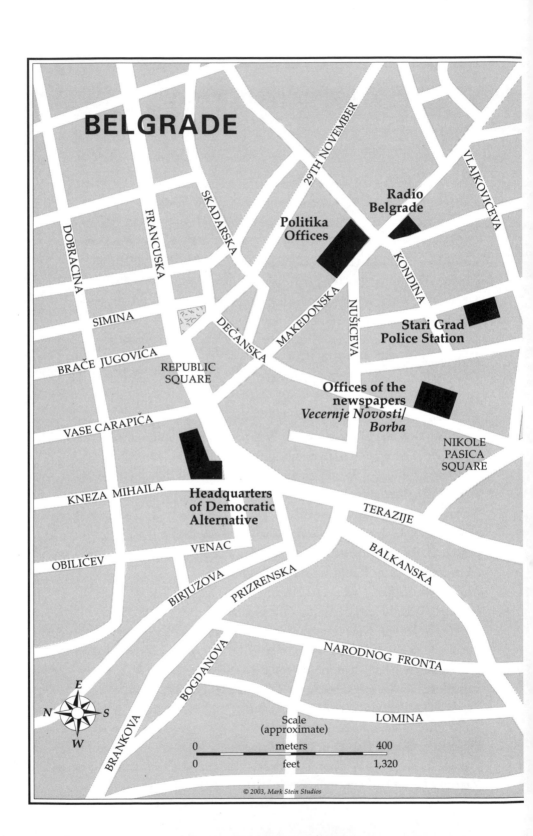

BELGRADE

29TH NOVEMBER

VLAJKOVIĆEVA

Radio
Belgrade

SKADARSKA

FRANCUSKA

Politika
Offices

KONDINA

DOBRACINA

MAKEDONSKA

NUŠIĆEVA

Stari Grad
Police Station

SIMINA

DEĆANSKA

BRAČE JUGOVIĆA

REPUBLIC
SQUARE

Offices of the
newspapers
*Vecernje Novosti/
Borba*

NIKOLE
PASICA
SQUARE

VASE CARAPIĆA

KNEZA MIHAILA

**Headquarters
of Democratic
Alternative**

TERAZIJE

BALKANSKA

VENAC

OBILIĆEV

BIRJUZOVA

PRIZRENSKA

BOGDANOVA

NARODNOG FRONTA

BRANKOVA

E
N ⊕ S
W

LOMINA

Scale
(approximate)

| 0 | meters | 400 |
| 0 | feet | 1,320 |

© 2003, Mark Stein Studios

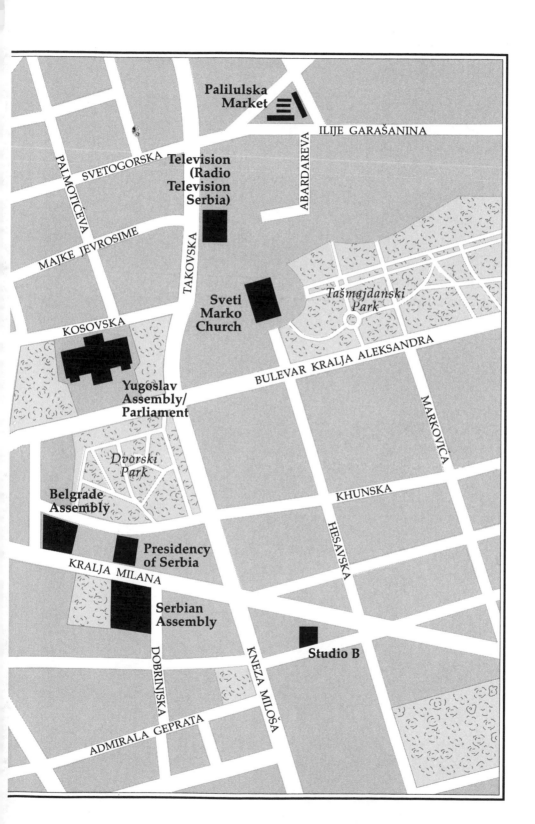